TRAINING YOUR DOG
THE HUMANE WAY

TRAINING YOUR DOG
THE HUMANE WAY

Simple Teaching Tips for
Resolving Problem Behaviors
& Raising a Happy Dog

ALANA STEVENSON

New World Library
Novato, California

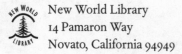

New World Library
14 Pamaron Way
Novato, California 94949

Interior photographs by Margaret Crow (www.margaretcrow.com), Kerri Fenn, Ed Friedman, Lauren MacDonald, and Lorraine Nicotera

Text design by Tona Pearce Myers

Library of Congress Cataloging-in-Publication Data
Stevenson, Alana.
 Training your dog the humane way : simple teaching tips for resolving problem behaviors and raising a happy dog / Alana Stevenson.
     p.   cm.
Includes bibliographical references and index.
ISBN 978-1-60868-018-4 (pbk.)
 1. Dogs—Training. 2. Dogs—Behavior. I. Title.
SF431.S74 2011
636.7'0835—dc22   2011006787

First printing, May 2011
ISBN 978-1-60868-018-4
Printed in Canada on 100% postconsumer-waste recycled paper

New World Library is a proud member of the Green Press Initiative.

10 9 8 7 6 5 4 3 2 1

1990–2002
This book is dedicated to Dolph Lundgren,
my beloved canine companion of many years.

Contents

Introduction

I WROTE THIS BOOK to give you an understanding of how dogs learn and interpret the world around them, at least when it comes to their interactions with us, and to provide you with the basic principles of teaching dogs humanely without the use of punishments, yelling, reprimands, or leash jerks. I hope that by writing this book, I will help you to understand your dogs better and to appreciate them for all their "dogginess" and intelligence.

Whatever your reasons for using this book, please be sure to read chapters 1 and 2 first. These chapters cover core concepts and key points, and will teach you how dogs learn, how behaviors are reinforced, and how to implement sound training techniques. After that, please refer to the table of contents and the index, and feel free to skip some chapters, focusing on those that address the topics most important to you and your dog. When practicing an exercise, first read through the section to get a feel for the whole lesson. Then follow the text as you would follow a recipe. If you have a partner, have her read the instructions as you work with your dog. (For the sake of convenience and consistency, I refer to all dogs as "he" and all humans as "she.") Do not skip steps or move on to new exercises too quickly. Make sure your dog masters the lesson before you proceed. I organized the lessons in such a way that they build on your dog's foundational skills. If your dog is a great listener and comes to you reliably but has difficulty staying or dropping objects for you, by all means, skim through the sections on the skills he has mastered, then jump to the sections on those that need work.

Working with your dog should be fun for both of you. There is a learning curve, however, so don't be too hard on yourself or your dog if the lessons seem cumbersome and awkward at first. Once you and your dog catch on, both of you will enjoy the "doggy-school game." Use extra good treats when teaching your dog, and always end with success — make sure your dog has accomplished the last task well and that you have told him what a brilliant doggy he is! Leave your dog wanting to learn more from you. This means that if your dog is having difficulty because you are moving too quickly or just because one of you is having a bad day, simply back up to a place where both of you are comfortable and reward your dog profusely for a job well done. Then release him and be happy. You can always go back to troubleshoot later.

Last, remember that learning with your dog should always be positive and enjoyable. Have fun with your lessons. Then, if you haven't already done so — take your dog for a walk! He's been waiting. (If you have a dog who resists going for walks or pulls excessively on the leash, check out chapter 6.)

Happy tails,

AS

Chapter One

POSITIVE TRAINING AND HOW DOGS LEARN AND UNDERSTAND THE WORLD AROUND THEM

WHAT IS POSITIVE TRAINING?

The term *positive training* means giving dogs rewards for what they do. A reward is something that your dog enjoys and that encourages him to repeat a behavior. Rewarding a dog can be done in many ways. Play, baby talk, smiling, food, praise, toys, petting, running, throwing grass for your dog to catch, swimming, walks, and tug-of-war can all tell your dog that what he is doing is good. Showing your dog that he has succeeded in learning what you were trying to teach is, in essence, positive training.

Positive training is a way of teaching your dog desired behaviors, redirecting and preventing unwanted behaviors, and encouraging your dog to work with you to achieve the best results in a positive, fun way — without frightening, bullying, inflicting pain, or physically forcing your dog to do what you want. Tools and techniques not used in positive training include choke, nylon slip, prong, pinch, or shock collars; jerking on the leash; squirting a dog with a water bottle; hitting; shaking a dog's scruff; kneeing a dog in the chest; slamming a dog to the ground; staring; growling; and yelling. (See appendix 4 for more information on harmful training techniques.) It is so much more enjoyable to compassionately teach your dog what you want from him than it is to be angry at him for not living up to your expectations.

WHY THERE IS NO NEED FOR PUNISHMENT

There is never any need for punishment. Animals don't entirely understand it (at least not when it comes from humans). They also become easily inhibited, shy, frightened, or agitated by punishment and may lose their love of play, along with a big portion of their self-esteem. Besides having these negative and damaging side effects, punishment does not give a dog the information he needs to succeed. It does not provide a dog with the knowledge necessary to do what the punisher is wanting. It only confuses the dog and creates more anxiety for him.

Another problem with "correction" and punishment-based training (such as using leash jerks, choke chains, pinch collars, physical confrontation, scolding, and reprimands to achieve desired results) is that animals do not learn well under stress. The moment any animal, including a human being, is stressed, his or her ability to learn decreases. Through positive methods, play, and motivation, you can teach your dog to overcome fear and anxiety and to learn behaviors on cue (in response to requests such as "Leave it," "Wait," "Drop," "Come," "Lie down," and "Stay") without making him anxious in the process.

DOGS ARE SOCIAL:
THEY DO EVERYTHING TOGETHER

Dogs are innately social and communal animals. They live, sleep, eat, play, and hunt together. It is psychologically stressful and abnormal for a dog to be left alone. Even if a dog is not in close proximity to another dog, he will usually remain in view of other dogs or follow them. This can be very problematic for dog owners who have only one dog, who want their dogs to sleep in a different room, or who work long hours.

This desire for social interaction and attention is why dogs will follow the people they are closest to from room to room (the so-called Velcro dogs). It is why, when left alone, many dogs do not want to eat and may panic. It is why dogs want to sleep on the bed with you and why puppies cry when you leave them. Even eating is communal. Your dog wants to eat with you and be close to you. This is why your dog may bring food from the kitchen into the living room and eat it while watching you watch television.

DOGS EXPERIENCE LIFE IN THE PRESENT

Dogs experience life in the present, as do most animals. They just go with the flow, interacting with and reacting to their environment as things happen to them. They are in the moment. This is a very innocent state.

We can catch a glimpse of what it is like to live in the moment by considering human infants and toddlers. Young toddlers learn what is safe versus dangerous, pleasant versus unpleasant. Their frustrations, anguish, hunger, and excitement all take place in the present. They don't think of the consequences of their actions or how past events affect future circumstances. Nor do they initially understand how your behaviors relate to theirs. And so it is with your canine companion.

Being in the present does not mean that your dog does not remember the past. Dogs, like other animals, remember past events, people, and places. If they didn't, they wouldn't know where to find their food bowl, who you were when you came home, what the leash meant when you picked it up, or where they left their favorite toy. But being in the moment means that they do not understand how your behavior in the present relates to their behaviors in the past.

This means a number of things when it comes to how dogs learn and interpret our behaviors. For example, if you are interacting with your dog because of something that happened four hours ago, he will not understand. He may remember what happened a few hours in the past but cannot relate your present behavior to a past event. This is another reason why punishing a dog is not very helpful. When you reprimand your dog for something he did in the past, he will not make the connection. He will assume that something is going on in the present that is unfortunate and potentially frightening. Likewise, if you interact with him regarding something that happened four seconds ago, he will most likely correlate your behavior with what is occurring at the present second.

In dog training, the success or failure of teaching a dog a concept or behavior depends on timing. Sometimes, to be effective, you must reinforce a behavior within a half second. If you are off by even a few seconds, your dog may be very confused about what you are trying to teach him. As the seconds pass, so does his understanding.

Unfortunately, by imagining our dogs as people, we set them up to fail to meet our expectations. We assume that they understand much more than they do. Living in the moment is much easier for us to observe than to conceptualize when teaching dogs. When you positively teach a dog a prompted (or cued) behavior, you realize quite quickly just how precise your timing has to be for him to understand you. You also realize how important your behaviors are in influencing your dog's behaviors.

DOGS ARE VISUAL, NOT VERBAL

Dogs learn visually, at least when it comes to their interactions with humans. It is much easier to teach a dog with hand signals, mannerisms, facial expressions, and body language than it is to teach him with verbal instruction. Tone of voice also affects how dogs learn and respond to people. Inflection is very important, since dogs tune in to sounds and noises that go up and down (such as a whistle or an expression such as "Hey" or "Let's go"), as opposed to the monotonous sound we make when we pronounce words like "Come," "Stand," "No," or "Stop."

Dogs do not easily discriminate among human words. Most of the time dogs are not paying attention to what we're saying, so when we talk to our dogs and then talk to each other, dogs tune us out. When you think your dog is tuning you out, you are probably right. This is not because your dog is purposely trying to ignore you, challenge you, or be stubborn; rather, it is because often he is simply focusing on other things and not on verbal language, especially language coming from another species! Of course, dogs can learn certain words and some aspects of what we say, but that long-winded dialogue you are having with your dog more than likely is going right over his head (that is, if you are expecting him to take you literally).

Using visual signals is the best way to teach a dog quickly and easily. Dogs are sensitive to your body language, the inflection and tone of your voice, your touch, and your proximity. Focus on enhancing your nonverbal communication skills, and your dog will be happy you did!

BODY LANGUAGE IS VERY MEANINGFUL TO DOGS

Body language is important to dogs. The way dogs position themselves in relation to one another has significance. If dogs are being friendly, they usually do not face each other directly. They position themselves parallel to each other or so that they are standing, sitting, or lying down at perpendicular angles to each other.

FIGURE 1.
Jake and Bessie
walking side by
side.

FIGURE 2. Jake and
Bessie positioning
themselves perpen-
dicularly — or at a
"T" — to each other.

Direct, face-to-face contact is very intense and stressful for most dogs. If dogs face each other and stare, a fight may ensue, especially if one dog fails to angle himself. Mock attacks during play, when one dog directly charges or faces another, are just for fun. But if this positioning is not preceded by play gestures such as paw taps and play-bows, the other dog will take it much more seriously.

Most of us approach dogs face on. We pet them directly on

top of their heads. We lean over and stare at them. When dogs approach us, we rarely angle ourselves away from them. Doing so would be a nice, welcoming gesture. When we face dogs directly and extend our hands toward them to pet their heads, we think we are being friendly, but many dogs get a different impression.

Many dogs become aggressive, or cower and seem head shy when people lean over them, pet them directly on the head, or stare at them while putting their faces too close to theirs. That's because these gestures and behaviors are threatening and unnerving to dogs. Some dogs learn to adapt to our body language, but others do not. Many canine behavior problems stemming from fear and aggression diminish considerably when people stop facing dogs directly and staring at them.

FIGURE 3. Kneeling perpendicularly — or at a "T" — to Kiva.

FIGURE 4. Perpendicular and parallel body language.

DOGS HAVE AN OPPOSITIONAL REFLEX

Dogs love tug-of-war because they have an oppositional reflex. That is, when dogs feel a force pushing against them or pulling on them, they will instinctively push or pull in the opposite direction. Have you ever noticed that when your dog approaches you and you push him away, he gets more excited and keeps pushing himself toward you? Or that the more you pull back on the leash, the more your dog seems to pull against you? When you push your dog down for jumping on you, you are actually encouraging him to jump back up because he is instinctively going against the force you exerted.

For this reason, you should not push him away from you when he jumps on you, close his mouth if he is play-biting, or pull back on the leash if he is pulling, or you will make the problem much worse. (For tips on preventing and eliminating play-biting and jumping, see chapter 4.)

DOGS DO NOT RESPECT PROPERTY RIGHTS: OWNERSHIP CHANGES PAWS

If an item is in a dog's mouth or under his paws, it is rightfully his. If nobody possesses an object, it is up for grabs. Dogs view ownership much the same way that toddlers do. If an item of yours is not in your possession, meaning that you are not actively holding, focusing on, or eating the object, then it is not your property.

FIGURE 5. Kiva running with her ball she found in the park.

Dogs don't naturally understand human property rights. In dog culture, if a dog does not let go of an item or walk away from it, it rightfully belongs to him. When a dog stops focusing on an object or becomes distracted and walks away from an object, another dog will take possession of it. *Ownership of an object changes according to who has it in the moment.*

Unless they live in the same household or know each other well, dogs normally do not remove items directly from other dogs' mouths. Doing so is rude, improper doggy etiquette. Fights can ensue when it is unclear to whom an item belongs, such as when two dogs approach an object at the same time. This is also why dogs may growl at people when people approach items that the dogs love. Dogs are saying, "Back off." It doesn't matter if it is your wallet, your cell phone, your underwear, or your socks. If your dog has it, it's his. It doesn't belong to you anymore.

AN OBJECT'S WORTH IS BASED ON ITS USE AND SOCIAL VALUE

The importance of an object to a dog is partly based on its use and social value to others. Tissues, socks, underwear, the TV remote, and stuffed toys in the children's rooms are all items that are important, novel, and used frequently. The old toy on the floor designated for the dog that nobody uses has little value, so your dog rarely plays with it. By having a toy bin, and playing with or acting interested in your dog's toys and other items you want your dog to have, your dog will be more enthusiastic about wanting those items too. If you chase your dog around the living room every time he grabs the Kleenex or toilet paper roll, you are only making the toilet paper roll or tissue more desirable to him.

DOGS LEARN BY ASSOCIATION

Animals learn by association. *Webster's New World Dictionary* defines *association* as "a connection in the mind between ideas, sensations, memories, etc." Dogs make connections by pairing events or sensations that occur simultaneously.

Not understanding that dogs learn this way can cause a lot of misunderstandings and lead to many behavioral problems in our dogs. For instance, if you jerk on the leash every time your dog sees a person, he will think that the next time he sees someone, he will be jerked or yanked. You might think you are correcting an unwanted behavior, such as jumping, barking, or lunging. Your dog, however, has not made this connection. He may assume that every time a person passes, you will jerk on his leash or punish him. Over time, he may establish a negative association with people and become fearful, aggressive, or overly submissive. This can happen if you punish your dog around other dogs, children, motorcyclists, bicyclists, skateboarders, or guests at the door. As a result of your frequent reprimands, scolding, and punishments, your dog now reacts to these triggers more frequently and with less provocation.

Why contribute more stress or anxiety to a situation your dog already feels upset or nervous about? Getting angry at your dog for being upset, anxious, or stressed out is, of course, not the best way to teach him to calm down. You will find that you can change many of your dog's fearful or negative emotions by desensitizing him (see chapter 5 for more about this technique) and by pairing positive things your dog enjoys with things he dislikes or finds unpleasant.

DOGS LEARN IN THE ENVIRONMENT
IN WHICH YOU TEACH THEM

Dogs learn in the context in which you teach them. If you teach your dog a behavior in the kitchen, he will think the behavior is linked to the kitchen. If you always teach him a behavior in the living room and assume he will perform the behavior in the hallway or on the patio when friends are over, he will probably disappoint you. You didn't teach him the behavior in the hallway or on the patio — you always taught him the behavior in the living room!

You have to teach a behavior in the environment in which you want it to occur. When training your dog, remember that when you change environments, you may have to reteach him what you think he already knows. Ultimately, you must teach your dog in the setting where you would like him to perform the behavior.

DOGS LEARN BY REPETITION, AND PRACTICE MAKES PERFECT

Dogs learn through repetition. The more often they engage in a certain behavior, the more likely they are to repeat it. Positive or negative, behavior patterns are likely to become habits. Practice makes perfect! If your dog performs a behavior once, the likelihood of his performing the behavior again is almost 100 percent. Be aware of this, and try to divert any unwanted behaviors before they become patterns.

SUMMARY

Positive Training and How Dogs Learn
and Understand the World around Them

- Dogs are social. They do everything communally.
- The use of punishments can make dogs fearful, anxious, and reactive.
- Dogs live in the moment. They do not understand how your present behavior relates to a past event. Nor are they contemplating the future or trying to usurp your power.
- Dogs are visual learners. Using your body language, visual signals, and voice inflection is the best way to teach dogs quickly and easily.
- When being friendly, dogs will position themselves so that they are at an angle to each other, or they will stand, lie down, or sit next to each other.

- To dogs, property rights are determined by who has immediate possession of an item. If a dog has an object of yours, he does not consider it your property anymore.
- The value of an object to a dog is based partially on its worth and importance to others.
- Dogs learn by association, that is, by pairing things that occur simultaneously in the environment.
- Dogs are context learners: they associate a new behavior with the environment in which you teach it to them. Ultimately, you must teach dogs in the settings in which you would like them to perform the behavior.
- Practice makes perfect. Dogs learn by repetition. Repeated behaviors are likely to become habits.

Chapter Two

TRAINING TECHNIQUES

PASSIVE TRAINING AND TEACHING BEHAVIORS

Passive training is a wonderful form of training that teaches us patience and gives dogs rewarding opportunities to learn what we want them to do. Passive training is a good way to teach fearful and timid dogs, is nonthreatening to aggressive dogs, and is friendly and unintimidating to submissive dogs. It is a great way to get a dog to look to you for guidance and to get his mental wheels turning.

Essentially, *passive training* is waiting for a behavior that your dog naturally exhibits (even if only for a moment) and then reinforcing that behavior by rewarding it. It means having the patience to wait for a desired behavior and then instantly reinforcing it through a reward and/or kudos the moment the behavior is performed. Through passive training, dogs learn that they get what they want when they do what you like. You can passively train polite manners and behaviors in many ways. But you always want to set your dog up for success.

Let's say your dog wants to go outside. The moment you open the door, he rushes past you and almost topples you. You can reward him for charging or jumping at the door or for backing away from it and waiting. If, as you open the door, he jumps on the door or charges past you and you let him out, you are reinforcing that behavior. On the other hand, if you wait for him to settle down before you open the door, he will learn that you open doors for him when he is calm and waiting. If you close the door whenever he charges for it or jumps on it, he will learn to wait politely for your okay when he wants you to open the door.

As you teach your dog to wait patiently for the door to open, the scenario may look like this: Your dog wants to go outside and bounces up and down enthusiastically as you begin to open the door. Instead of opening the door, you wait. For an instant he stops jumping and looks at you, so you begin to open the door. He begins to dash out. You close the door before he has the opportunity. Your dog is surprised and backs up a step. He may look at you and wait for a moment. You begin to open the door again, and again he charges the door. Before he gets out, you close it again. Your dog, a bit perplexed and frustrated, stops jumping and looks at you. This time he may remain staring at you for a few seconds. You smile (showing that he is doing what you want) and begin to open the door again. He hesitates and then begins to charge the door. You close the door the instant he begins to make a run for it. Eventually, stupefied, he looks at you and waits patiently. He hesitates when you open the door, looks at you, and waits. "Okay, great job!" you say, and immediately let him outside.

You have now just reinforced and rewarded waiting as a behavior for getting the door to open. You can then add refinements if you wish. You can teach your dog to walk to the door, make eye contact with you, and sit. Voilà! The door opens. Of course, you can also just open the door and let your dog run exuberantly by. Just don't get angry at him for behaving in a way that you've been reinforcing.

The above is an example of passive training. A few repetitions, and your dog will begin to figure out that when he is calm and not jumping at the door, you will open it for him. When he jumps or charges at the door, you close it. He wants the door to open, so eventually he will wait politely by the door while you open it. No other behavior seems to make you open the door. You could order your dog to sit, push his bottom down, get frustrated, or yell at him for jumping or charging at the door. Alternatively, through passive training you can teach him from the start that all the goodies in life, such as doors being opened, leashes being removed, cookies, pats, belly rubs, the right to jump on the sofa, and playing with the tug toy, come by way of showing polite manners. The moment your dog stops behaving politely, or starts behaving in a way you dislike, you stop giving him the goodies.

Gentleness, kindness, praise, baby talk, walks, food, playing with other dogs, playing with balls or toys, car rides, running, attention, and the right to be on the bed are all things that your dog desires and finds rewarding. If you reward him by giving him these things when he acts out (such as when he exhibits hyperactive or overly zealous mouthy or jumpy behaviors), he will continue to act out. Why? Because you reinforce and reward these behaviors.

We often unintentionally reinforce attention-seeking behaviors. Being social creatures, dogs think that any attention — as long as it is not intensely negative — is better than no attention at all. To get your attention, which means making eye contact and interacting with you, your dog will exhibit a behavior that produces a reaction. If your dog engages in this behavior and you look at him (if only for a second), reprimand him, or focus on the behavior in any way, you reinforce it. Your dog wanted your attention, and you just gave it to him. He will do whatever works and will keep doing it, even if you hate it.

On the other hand, if your dog performs a behavior that you don't like in order to get your attention, and you immediately remove all eye contact and disengage from him, he will find another way to get your attention. This, of course, puts the responsibility on your shoulders. Does biting you in the butt work to get your attention, or will you respond to him if he is calm or well-mannered?

We tend to focus on behaviors that we dislike in our dogs and to ignore the behaviors that we like. When a dog does exactly what we want, we often overlook it. We are relieved that he didn't do something we dislike. The moment that he performs a behavior that we find annoying, problematic, emotionally draining, or frightening — barking, for instance — we reinforce this behavior by interacting with him. Reverse your tendency to obsess over and focus on the things that disturb you about your dog. React to him when he shows behaviors that you like. They are there — you just might be missing them. When your dog is quiet, you can gently say, "Good quiet," and pet him to acknowledge him for being quiet, *before* he begins barking. When your dog doesn't lunge at the car, you can acknowledge and reward him for being calm and looking at you instead. If your dog does not growl at you for walking by his bone while he is eating it, you can praise him and give him a treat.

A well-behaved, happy dog usually has a proactive, observant human guardian. (Or the person is very fortunate to have a dog who is well-behaved regardless of her actions!) Obviously, humane training requires patience and respect for your dog. Passive training is a way to reward and focus on behaviors that you like without verbally or physically instructing your dog to exhibit them. Your dog figures out the behaviors that you want on his own. These behaviors will soon become his default behaviors, if they are reinforced consistently.

SHAPING A BEHAVIOR

Shaping a behavior means achieving and reinforcing a behavior incrementally. Your dog may not show the exact behavior you are looking for, but at times he does exhibit behavior resembling the one you wish to see. Shaping means reinforcing any behavior closely resembling the behavior that you are looking for. Reinforcement means giving your dog something that will make him want to perform the behavior again. Food is a great reinforcer for many dogs and is easy to work with.

Successive approximation is the best way to shape a behavior. You reward your dog for exhibiting a behavior that closely resembles the behavior you want. The closer the initial behavior resembles the desired behavior, the more you reward your dog. This means you give him more treats, or you give him rewards that are more valuable to him. You can then ask or encourage him to show you more of that behavior. He will perform initial behaviors that resemble the end behaviors you want. Eventually, through shaping and gradual reinforcement with successive approximations, he will perform the desired final behavior.

Think of successive approximations as getting closer to a goal. Imagine that you were blindfolded and had to locate an object. At times you are closer to it and at times farther away. If someone watched you, praising and rewarding you every time you were closer to the item, you would gradually be shaped to locate the item by successive approximations. The more feedback and encouragement you were given, the more quickly and easily you would be able to accomplish the task.

Complex behaviors such as heeling, weaving between your legs, turning on and off a light switch, retrieving, and putting toys in a toy basket can all be shaped. Teaching a dog to walk closely next to you, to stay by your side, and to stop and turn when you do, is teaching a high-level behavior. A dog has to learn many steps and sequences in order to heel or walk next to you. Dogs cannot learn to heel in one step like they can learn to sit on cue. Making eye contact, taking a step when you take a step, walking adjacent to you, stopping, turning with you — both to the right and to the left — are all separate behaviors that need to be taught individually to your dog.

When you break down a behavior such as heeling into its components, you see that it isn't so simple. To teach your dog properly, you need to be aware of all the individual behaviors that he needs to learn. If you do not build on a foundation, you and your dog will get lost as you try to progress.

When you teach a dog to heel by using a choke collar, you do not teach him to voluntarily walk next to you, look at you, turn with you, or stay to one side of you. Instead, you physically force him to stay by your side. To really learn a behavior, a dog must be able to choose that behavior from a range of alternatives. When you use a choke collar on your dog, he cannot choose one behavior over another. You cannot reinforce a behavior if there is only one behavior to reinforce.

If your dog is on a choke collar and he proceeds ahead of you, he is jerked on his trachea. If he lags behind, he is tugged by a chain around his neck to make him catch up. "Leash pops" are serious business. They are painful and constrict a dog's airway. He will learn to avoid the jerk by staying next to your leg. From his perspective, this is the only option. He is not walking with you voluntarily, nor does he desire to look to you for guidance or direction. Those who rely on the choke collar and think that their dogs have learned how to walk next to them off-leash should remove the choke chain and see whether their dogs can do so. If they do, do these dogs really want to stay by their owners' sides, or are they staying there because they are afraid of getting hurt?

You can shape many behaviors that you want your dog to exhibit. Fetching, for instance, is a behavior that can be shaped in a dog not accustomed to playing. If your dog seems to go after a ball but does not want to bring the ball back, you can shape the behavior of retrieving. As he runs to the ball, praise him and maybe give him a treat. When he leaves the ball, ignore him. If he then proceeds back to the ball, reward him and encourage him through praise and positive feedback every step of the way. This is an example of passive training. Eventually, he may mouth the object. You can reward him even more. By the time he learns to pick up the toy, you can then teach him to carry it and drop it in your direction. Over time, you can teach him to carry the object and drop it on cue. Then you can reward him for dropping the object closer and closer to you, until finally he can drop the object in your hand.

Shaping a behavior is a good way to work with dogs without putting so much pressure on them that they fail to engage in the final behavior. If a behavior consists of many smaller foundational steps, dogs cannot be expected to perform the end desired behavior the right way on the first try.

We tend to correct dogs for performing unwanted behaviors before they even know what is expected of them. Focus on rewarding and reinforcing any behaviors that you want. Ignore those behaviors that you wish to discourage. If you focus on unwanted behaviors, you will just distract your dog with irrelevant information, and that will set you both up for failure. It is like teaching a child arithmetic. A child cannot learn how to add if the teacher focuses only on the child's mistakes and wrong answers. Focus on what your dog does right. You will find that those behaviors increase in frequency. Your dog will be much happier too!

LURING

Luring is what most people think of as bribing a dog. Often people fail to get beyond the luring stage during training and then criticize the technique. However, luring is a very important part of positive training. Luring involves getting a dog to follow an object, including food. By teaching a dog to follow an item, you can build on several foundational steps, move him through various positions, and teach him to execute a desired behavior.

Dogs are visual and will usually start to focus on your hand or the object you are holding. You can then turn any motion that you used to lure the dog into a hand signal or verbal instruction. By having your dog follow something, whether it is food, a tennis ball, or a squeaky toy, you can move his body into certain positions or prompt him to follow a certain pattern. By moving him through the use of lures, you can teach him a sequence or position change without *physical prompting*, which is using physical force to move a dog into a position. Pushing on a dog's shoulder blades to make him lie down is an example of physical prompting. Pulling him on a leash to make him come to you is another example.

Luring will produce better results. Wherever you move the lure, your dog follows. Once he gets the idea, you can wean him off the lure by making it less visually obvious to him and then rewarding him in other ways, such as offering him something in addition to, or instead of, the lure, or by varying the rewards you give him. Eventually you can wean him off the lure entirely. Your dog follows a verbal prompt or a hand signal (or both), and you give him a reward that will make him repeat the behavior. Food is just one of many rewards you can use. A reward is anything your dog likes or finds fun to do.

FIGURE 6.
Luring a sit.

There is a difference between bribing and luring. A good example of bribing is teaching a dog to sit for cookies. People hold up a cookie and say, "Sit," and the dog sits (which he will do because when dogs look up, their bottoms eventually hit the floor), and then they give the dog the cookie. When people are not asking the dog to sit, they are usually not showing the dog a cookie. People routinely give cookies for sitting. Most dogs figure out quite quickly that when their heinies hit the ground, cookies appear.

However, if we teach dogs to sit for cookies, we usually fail to teach them to sit while we are opening doors or putting on or taking off leashes. We assume that dogs know what to do or how to sit because we taught them how to sit when they see cookies. But if you've never taught your dog to sit while you put on the leash, open a door, or throw a ball, he will never learn and most likely will not understand what you are requesting of him.

Using a lure can help move your dog into a sitting position. You can then ask him to sit by using a lure while you put on his leash. While you put on the leash, you can reward him with the cookie you used to lure him. Then you can wean him off cookies. The leash and then a walk outside become the reward. If you do not visually wean him off the lure, he will have a tough time doing the behavior without seeing it. Your dog doesn't have to become a food junkie to be positively taught with food.

ACTIVE TRAINING

Active training is what most people picture when they think of dog training: the use of a lure, prompt, or cue to encourage a dog to exhibit a desired behavior. Active training is the opposite of passive training. Passive training is when you wait for the dog to perform the behavior on his own and then reinforce the behavior by rewarding him. Both techniques are used in humane training.

The next chapter covers some basic exercises that will help you teach your dog positively and have fun at the same time. The aid of an experienced, qualified, positive trainer may help you learn these exercises more quickly. Although positive trainers share many of the same principles, every trainer has her own style and methods. In the back of this book, you will find a section on how to choose a trainer both you and your dog will like.

SUMMARY

Training Techniques

- Passive training means waiting for a behavior that your dog naturally exhibits — even if only for a moment — and then reinforcing that behavior by rewarding it. It involves having the patience to wait for a desired behavior and then instantly reinforcing it through rewards and/or praise the moment it happens.
- Passive training is especially good for fearful, timid, submissive, and aggressive dogs.
- Attention-seeking behaviors are motivated by the desire for eye contact and interaction with you.
- If you reinforce a behavior, it will be repeated.
- Shaping a behavior means achieving and reinforcing behavior incrementally.
- Successive approximation is the best way to shape a behavior.
- Complex behaviors, such as heeling, weaving between your legs, turning a light switch on and off, dropping and retrieving objects, and putting toys in a toy basket can all be shaped.
- Shaping a behavior is a good way to work with dogs without putting so much pressure on them that they fail to achieve the desired final behavior.
- Luring means getting a dog to follow an object, including food. By teaching dogs to follow an object, you can then move them into different positions and teach them to perform specific behaviors.

- By getting dogs to move through the use of lures, you can teach them a sequence or position change without physical prompting. You can then teach them to perform these behaviors by following hand signals or verbal prompts.
- Physical force does not teach a dog to trust you or to look to you for guidance. It only intimidates him or makes him fear you.
- Active training is using a lure, prompt, or cue to encourage a dog to perform a behavior. In active training, you use physical, verbal, or visual instruction to prompt dogs to perform specific behaviors.

A NOTE ON TEACHING PUPPIES

There is no special consideration specifically to be given to puppies that should not or cannot be given to older dogs. In general, puppies have shorter attention spans than older dogs. Young puppies especially can be easily distracted. They are also less coordinated than young adult or older dogs and may require more time to learn skills. Short, frequent training sessions are more productive than long ones. In other words, a puppy might enjoy three to fifteen minutes of training, followed by some playtime. Puppies are not good at endurance and require frequent bouts of play, eating, sleep, and mental stimulation.

Not all older dogs can pay attention for long periods. Conversely, some puppies can fixate on something of interest for up to an hour. However, the rule for all positive training is to leave the dog or puppy wanting more. It is more effective to incorporate training into your day and to have fifteen two- to six-minute training sessions than it is to have one thirty-minute training session.

There is no reason to wait before teaching a puppy. An eight-week-old puppy can certainly learn to come, look at you, leave

FIGURE 7. Puppies do best with short, frequent training sessions, followed by play, eating, or sleeping.

objects, sit, and give you a toy. When taught positively, he will love doing so. Your puppy is learning from you, whether or not you think you are teaching him anything. He is looking to you for guidance. It is wise to set him up for success early on. Remember to be happy and positive when teaching dogs, especially puppies.

Puppies should be fed three meals a day. Some people tend to underfeed puppies, fearing their puppy might gain too much weight. Puppies are little calorie-burning machines. If your puppy seems frantic or hungry for food or treats, or becomes obsessive or hyper when you are eating, he may need to eat more. Sometimes excess hyperactivity can be caused because your puppy is too hungry. Giving bigger, regular meals will help puppies relax and settle down.

You can teach and train your puppy with doggy kibble, but stay away from heavily processed food or treats with artificial colors and a lot of by-products. Avoid food containing sugar, corn syrup, and cornmeal. Instead, stick with treats that contain grains, such as oats or brown rice. Fresh veggies and fruit can also be used as treats for puppies. Avoid feeding puppies too much variety at one time. Do not feed your dog grapes, raisins, onions, or chocolate.

Chapter Three

TEACHING THE BASICS

TEACHING A RELEASE WORD

Teaching your dog a release word is easy to do and will make your instructions much clearer to him. A release word conveys to your dog that there is a transition and that he no longer has to engage in the behavior you were requesting of him.

People often ask their dogs to sit but then fail to release them by giving their dogs a clear signal. Then they become frustrated when their dogs stand up or get distracted. It is unfair to expect your dog to do a behavior indefinitely, nor will he be able to. Teaching your dog a release word eliminates this confusion.

To teach your dog a release word, reward him for doing a behavior, then say "Okay," "No more," or "That's it." Praise and pet your dog, then disassociate from him by removing all eye contact. Alternatively, you can engage him in another behavior, such as running with you, playing with a toy, or chasing a stick. The release word indicates a transition.

You can choose different release words for different contexts. For instance, if your dog is playing in the park, ask him to perform a behavior for you, and then release him to "Go play." When you are finished massaging or brushing your dog, say, "No more" or "That's it," pet and praise him, and then engage him in another activity, or walk away from him and do something he has no interest in. Before you cross a street, praise your dog for waiting with you. Then say, "Okay" or "Let's go" to let him know to walk with you again.

GETTING YOUR DOG'S ATTENTION

Getting your dog's attention is very important. If you can't get his attention, you won't get much else. Frequently, we call our dogs by their names and make eye contact with them, then lose the connection. When you call your dog's name, he will look at you, but then he will look away and continue to do what he was previously doing. When he is looking at you, he is asking, "What do you want?" If you miss or don't acknowledge his eye contact, he will think that you didn't know what you wanted or that his name doesn't mean anything.

Getting your dog's attention means that when you can call him by his name, he looks at you or in your direction. This behavior can be shaped and is particularly good for dogs who are afraid of making eye contact or who avoid eye contact entirely. It is also an important behavior to shape for a good *recall* (getting your dog to come to you when called).

Do's

- Do call your dog by his name only when you have his attention or know you will get it. Don't set yourself up for failure by becoming a broken record.

- Do use your dog's name in a positive way. If he senses stress or frustration, he may avoid making eye contact.
- Do use inflection when trying to get your dog's attention. Noises that naturally get dogs' attention are high-pitched and varied (such as whistles, claps, and smoochy kisses).
- Do make calling your dog's name relevant to him. When he hears his name, something should follow that relates to him. You could kiss him, throw him a ball, show him the keys indicating he is going for a car ride, ask him to sit, run away from him to entice him to come to you, and so on. But you must follow through with an instruction or an activity. Remember, his name is his identity; it doesn't give him any instructions.
- Do say your dog's name more loudly and more clearly, and add some noises or sounds, if you cannot get his attention. If you *still* cannot get his attention, keep trying by making yourself more interesting or exciting, or go get him, but do *not* use his name. The more you repeat his name while he ignores you, the less likely it will be that he pays attention to you.

Don'ts

- Don't try to get your dog's attention by using his name unless you are fairly certain to get it.
- Don't use your dog's name as a replacement for the instruction "Come." His name simply means "Hey you!" It does not provide him with any information.
- Don't use your dog's name when you mean to say "No." Just as a dog's name does not mean "Come," it also does not mean "No."
- Don't use your dog's name in a negative context or when

you are angry. He will avoid making eye contact in an effort to appease you, and he may become anxious on hearing his name.

• Don't repeat your dog's name over and over again hoping for a different result if you cannot get his attention by calling his name after a few tries. By repeating his name incessantly, you will desensitize him to it, and he will ignore you. Try using other ways to get his attention.

ATTENTION EXERCISES

The following two exercises, the Check-In and Focus on Me, shape eye contact and establish a positive association for your dog as you look at each other. Once you can visually cue him to make eye contact, you can add a verbal prompt by pairing it with his behavior. He will learn that this prompt means to look at you.

The Check-In

The Check-In is fairly simple to teach. Start in a quiet room with few distractions. Have a treat ready. Hold the treat behind your back. Do not look at your dog. Ignore him. Wait for him to be mildly distracted or to look away from you. He might glance in another direction, sniff the ground, or begin to walk away from you. The moment he turns his head away from you, make a high-pitched, enticing noise. This noise should have inflection and be something you consistently use to get your dog's attention. Designate a sound like "Hey" or a whistle, or make a clicking noise with your tongue. The noise should be interesting enough that your dog glances in your direction or looks at you. The moment your dog looks at you or turns his head toward you, give him the treat you have been holding behind your back. Praise him. Then repeat the exercise.

When he catches on to the game, begin adding distractions. Wait for your dog to be mildly distracted. Make your sound, and then give him a treat for looking at you. If he does not look at you, get closer to him, make the sound louder, and/or vary the sounds you make. When he looks at you, praise and treat him. Continue practicing the Check-In exercise until you can get his attention in moderately or highly distracting areas. Always use better rewards in areas where there are more exciting or challenging distractions.

FIGURE 8. Rewarding and acknowledging Sebby for eye contact.

You need to reward your dog instantly so that he makes the connection between the sound you make and his eye contact. Pick at least two sounds you can practice with. You can also perform this exercise by using his name. By designating a few sounds to entice him to look at you, you are giving yourself more options if he fails to respond to his name. You want your dog to look at you or check in with you regularly, especially if you are outside; but if you keep repeating his name, you will desensitize him to it. Remember, his name should be followed by formal instruction or feedback. The sounds you designate for him to look at you simply encourage him to give you eye contact. You can reward him for looking at you without saying his name.

If you are struggling to get your dog's attention, practice rewarding your dog for looking at you, whether or not you request it. This is especially helpful on walks. Dogs frequently glance at us to check in with us or see what we are doing. When your dog looks at you, acknowledge it by praising and rewarding him. He will start looking at you more often.

Focus on Me (or Focused Attention)

Sit or kneel opposite your dog so that he is facing you. Give him a treat if he is sitting, although he does not have to sit for this exercise. Hold a food treat in your hand. Show him the treat, then draw your hand up toward your eyes. Position the treat so that it is in front of your nose. Pause there for a second or two. When he looks at you, treat him. Repeat this about ten to fifteen times.

FIGURE 9. Drawing Macey's attention to my face.

When this exercise seems easy and your dog seems delighted to play it, make the exercise more challenging. Show your dog the treat by positioning your hand approximately two inches from his nose, then draw the treat up to your face, placing your hand holding the treat just under your eye, near your cheekbone. When your dog looks you in the eye, give him the treat.

FIGURE 10. Macey looks in my eyes, and then I reward her.

When you feel that your dog is giving you good eye contact and is confident with the exercise, put your hand holding the treat two to six inches in front of your dog's nose, then bring that hand next to your head, with the tips of your fingers touching the back of your ear. Most dogs will initially look at the hand holding the food and not into your eyes. *Wait.* Do not prompt or encourage him to look at you. The instant he looks at you, give him the treat. This is passive training. Keep repeating this exercise until your dog readily looks at you and makes good eye contact with you.

Once your dog masters the exercise, increase the length of time he looks at you. Initially you are asking him to make eye contact with you for a few seconds. To increase the duration, simply delay giving the treat by one or two seconds. After your dog looks at you, he will naturally look back at the treat. This is okay. If your dog looks away too quickly, you may be going too fast or expecting too much from him. Once he can look at you and maintain eye contact for two seconds or longer, speak his name or say a word such as "Watch" or "Look" a second before signaling for eye contact. You can also use the noise you have designated for eye contact in the Check-In exercise.

If you have difficulty determining whether your dog is looking at you, move your hand a few inches away from your ear so you can see his eyes shift. Then keep your hand still. The object of the exercise is for your dog to focus on your eyes and not on your hand. If you move your hand too frequently, it will become distracting. (Note: If you are doing this exercise in a room with overhead lighting, the lighting can be distracting and can cast a reflection in your dog's eyes. Reposition yourself in the room so that you can see whether your dog is looking at you.)

Once your dog can perform the attention exercises in one room, change rooms. Then change locations. Do the exercises outside in a quiet setting. Change your body position. Ask for his attention while he is standing, sitting on the sofa, going for a walk, and so on. Always begin the exercises in an area with few distractions. When adding distractions or when outside, decrease the amount of time you ask him to look at you for, and remember to use more desirable rewards.

RECALL: TEACHING YOUR DOG TO COME TO YOU

A recall — training lingo for coming when called — takes place when your dog, after being away from you, approaches you again upon receiving a designated hand or verbal signal. You do not have to use the word "Come" as your recall signal. You can use another expression, such as "This way" or "Over here," or you can use a whistle.

There may be times when you have to physically go and get your dog. This is to be expected, but this is not a recall. Running after your dog and chasing him does not encourage him to come to you.

Do's

- Do teach your dog the meaning of your recall signal. Call him with your designated prompt or cue when he is already coming to you or when you know that he will approach you.

FIGURE 11. Calling Kiva to come as she retrieves teaches her the meaning of the recall signal.

- Do run or move away from your dog if you want him to come to you! His natural inclination will be to follow you. He will not learn to approach or follow you if you are chasing or following him.

FIGURE 12. Walking away from Macey encourages her to follow me.

- Do walk, move, and orient your body in the direction that you want your dog to go when following you. If you stop, stand still, or face him and watch what he is doing or looking at, he will be less likely to pay attention to you because you are not giving him any clear guidance or instruction.
- Do use high-pitched noises (such as baby talk, squeaks, whistles, smoochy kisses, and claps) and change the inflection in your voice to get your dog's attention. "Let's go" and "I'm leaving" are two expressions that go up and down in pitch as we say them. Dogs tend to tune out monotonous sounds.
- Do position yourself with your back angled toward your dog, kneel down, and call him if he is fearful, hesitant, or timid. A hesitant dog will approach you if he feels that you are not threatening. We face dogs when we want to block their movements or teach them to back away or to stay. If you do face your dog, walk or run away from him as

you call him, unless you are teaching him a formal recall through the training exercises. When he leaves you temporarily, he is not running away from you permanently but is preoccupied with something else. More than likely, he *will* want to come back to you. He just wants to do something else first. The more distractions there are in your dog's environment, the more enticing you have to be when you want him to come to you.

FIGURE 13. Kneeling away from Jake to encourage him to approach.

- Do encourage your dog the entire time he is in the process of coming to you. You can easily lose his interest as he approaches you. If you are too boring, he will find something else more stimulating to do.
- Do kneel down as your dog comes to you, and avoid leaning forward or reaching over him with outstretched arms, especially if he is fearful or shy.

- Do praise and reward your dog profusely when he gets to you. Rewards can be food or activities he enjoys, such as running or playing tug-of-war.
- Do call your dog to come to you, make his recall rewarding, and then release him by letting him go back to what he was doing previously. By releasing your dog after he has come to you and you have rewarded him, you are telling him that coming to you is a positive experience and not just a way to end play or to indicate that an activity he enjoys is over.

Don'ts

- Don't call your dog with your designated signal unless he is approaching you or you know he will come to you. If you repeatedly call him while he continues to ignore you, you will desensitize him to your signal.
- Don't chase or follow your dog if you want him to come to you.
- Don't stand still, face your dog, or lean directly over him, if you want him to come to you.
- Do not punish your dog for coming to you by using it as an opportunity to reprimand or scold him or to end social interactions or play.
- Do not call your dog with your signal if you are going to do something he doesn't like, such as clip his nails or give him a bath.

RECALL EXERCISES

The principles of recall can be taught through games that help your dog learn your signal. Be sure to use your "Come" signal in situations other than the games. If you use your signal only when playing the games, your dog will not generalize it to other situations. Remember, dogs learn in the environments and contexts in which you teach them.

I've included recall games for one, two, and three or more people. Once your dog is good at the one- and two-person recall games, you can vary the games as you see appropriate, or play the three-person games to further reinforce his recall. Always end games on a successful note so that your dog feels happy and confident in his abilities.

One-Person Games

Run Away from Your Dog

This game seems simple enough, but surprisingly few people practice running away from their dogs when they want their dogs to follow them. By running away from your dog, you encourage him to follow you. You can then add your recall signal every time you know he will come to you or catch up to you.

Have a few treats or hold a few toys of equal value that your dog loves. Stand still. Do not look at your dog. When your dog least expects it, run away from him, act excited, make high-pitched noises, and call your dog to come to you. When your dog runs after you, praise him, give him a treat, or toss the toy for him. You can also play tug-of-war with him. Treat him for releasing the toy, and then repeat the game.

When he comes to you happily, begin touching his collar before you give him a treat or throw him a toy. Then release him and repeat.

If you make this game fun and enjoyable, your dog will have a great time chasing you and following your lead.

Basic One-Person Recall

If you play this game on light surfaces, you will need dark treats, and vice versa. Your dog needs to be able to find the treats quickly and easily. If you play on grass or patterned carpets, he will have to spend too much time trying to find the treats. Play this game on hard surfaces, such as tile or wooden floors, sidewalks, driveways, or tennis courts.

Teach your dog a hand signal before you teach him the game. Your hand signal does not have to become a formal signal. You are simply going to use your hand as a target — something visual for your dog to follow.

To teach the hand signal, imagine a half-inch length of string running between your dog's nose and your hand. Wherever you move your hand, his nose should follow. With food in your hand, place the back of your hand toward your dog's nose, and lure him to you by pulling your hand toward your body. Once he gets to you, give him the treat. This will encourage him to come close to you. Do this until he can approach you by following your hand without a food lure. This is also a good opportunity to practice touching his collar. You can then treat him after you do so. Once he follows your hand without hesitation, begin the game.

Hold a bunch of treats in one hand behind your back or keep treats with you in a training pouch. Stand facing your dog. Roll a food treat on the floor about one foot away from you. Don't throw the treat over your dog's head, or he will lose track of it. When he gets the treat, hold another treat in your hand and lure him back to you. Instead of giving him the treat when he gets to you this time, praise him, and roll the treat about two feet away from you.

Continue to roll or toss the food treats, increasing the distance with each toss and luring your dog back to you each time with another treat. Believe it or not, when you throw a food treat, your dog will not immediately come back to you for more. Most dogs just sniff the ground, hoping more treats will rain from the sky. Once your dog understands the game and starts coming back to you after each toss without your having to lure him, add a verbal signal: his name followed by "Come" (or whatever word you have chosen as your "Come" signal). Say these words when he is almost done eating the food treat or has just finished. He will come to you after you call him. It will look as if he is listening to your verbal prompt, although at this point he is just following the rules of the game.

FIGURES 14, 15, 16. Playing the one-person basic recall game with Lucy: I toss a treat, she gets the treat and then comes to me, and I reward her by tossing a treat again.

Once your dog comes to you reliably after each toss, put your hands behind your back. Use only your verbal signal without luring him. If he is already looking at you and approaching you, you do not need to say his name. Just use your "Come" signal to reinforce the behavior. If he hesitates, lure him or entice him with your hand motion.

The purpose of this exercise is not to teach your dog to run after the food, but to teach him to come to you. If you throw the food too far away from you in the early stages of the game, or if you throw it before your dog has gotten back to you, he may not come back to you all the way after each throw. Wait for him to get to you before you throw the treat again. If he does not come to you, repeat his name and your "Come" signal once, add some prompts, and immediately use your hand signal to encourage him to come to you. Then praise him and toss the food treat when he comes to you.

If your dog plays fetch and can bring objects back to you and then release the object for you to throw again, you have a recall game! Call your dog by saying his name and your "Come" signal every time he gets the object and heads back in your direction.

Once your dog understands this game, play it in many different environments. Begin using your "Come" signal in real-life situations when he is at short distances from you. Follow a two-to-three call rule: Call your dog to come to you once. If he doesn't come, wait for a moment, then say his name more loudly and clearly, adding high-pitched noises. The instant he looks at you, run in the opposite direction or move in the direction in which you want him to follow you. If he does not come to you the second time you call, do whatever you can to get him to approach you. You may have to go to him and put the leash on him, but don't keep repeating his name or your "Come" signal. Otherwise, he will become desensitized to both.

Start preceding all enjoyable activities — when you know your dog will approach — with your designated "Come" signal. This will not only help to reinforce your signal, but it will also make coming to you a positive experience for him.

After you say your dog's name, do not wait too long before

adding your "Come" signal, or he will look at you but not know what you want from him. He will then quickly lose interest, and you will be forced to try to get his attention all over again.

Identical Toys

This is a good recall game for dogs who are motivated by balls and toys. It is also a nice game for dogs who do not carry toys around but like to chase them and for dogs who have not been taught to drop objects.

Use two or three identical toys that your dog loves, such as stuffed toys, tennis balls, or tug toys. Stand in the middle of an open area. If you do not want your dog off-leash, use a long line (extra-long lead). Show him a toy, and throw it for him. Just as he gets to the toy, get his attention and wave an identical toy. Then run away from him.

Enthusiastically call him to come to you using your designated signal. As soon as your dog reaches you, stop running, praise him, and throw the toy that you are holding in the opposite direction of that in which you threw the first toy. As he runs by you to get the newly thrown toy, pick up the toy you threw originally and wave it again, calling him to come to you using your designated signal. Keep repeating this pattern, calling him every time.

Once your dog learns this game, you can vary it by teaching him to drop the toy, so that he drops one toy right at your feet and then runs after a newly tossed toy. This game is a wonderful way to exercise your dog, reinforce a recall, and teach him a "Give," "Drop," or a "Thank-you" (giving him a treat for releasing a toy).

Two-Person Games

Since the one-person games teach a dog the body language and voice of the caller, it is best for both people playing the Basic

Two-Person Recall game to play the Basic One-Person Recall game with their dog first.

Basic Two-Person Recall

Have ready treats that your dog will enjoy. Stand about four feet away from your partner so you each can be within an arm's reach of your dog. Lure him to come to you with a food treat. When he comes to you, give him the treat. Then the other player steps in and lures your dog to come. When your dog goes to that person, she delivers a treat.

Once your dog understands the game and will run back and forth between players for food treats, add your verbal signal. Say his name and immediately follow it with your "Come" signal while you lure him to you with your hand motion or the treat. Increase the distance between you and your partner as your dog gets better at playing the game. When your dog catches on to the game, there will be no need to lure him. Then you can focus on your verbal signal. If your dog regresses and stops coming to you when you stop using your hand signal, decrease the distance between you and your partner. You may have stopped using your hand motion or the lure too soon. Also, if you increase the distance too quickly, a dog will usually stay by one person, and the game will deteriorate.

Once your dog understands that the game consists of running back and forth between two people for goodies, you will need a signal to let your partner know when it is her turn to call, especially when you are at a distance from each other or in locations where you can't see each other. Say a word or expression such as "Perfect" or "Good job" after you give your dog the food treat. This way, your partner will hear and know when it is her turn to call. Then you won't end up calling your dog at the same time or before any treats have been delivered. This additional verbal cue also lets your dog know that it is time to race back to the other person. Essentially, this cue is his release.

Do not repeat your dog's name or call him over and over again if he does not pay attention or come to you. Try a prompt, such as a whistle or a hand clap, and then use your hand signal to lure him to you.

FIGURES 17 and 18. Playing a two-person recall game.

Hide-and-Seek

Once your dog can play the above two-person game, you can play hide-and-seek with him. Your dog can get treats and be rewarded for finding people. When teaching your dog this game, don't make hiding places too difficult at first. "Hide" in a place where he can see you. Many dogs love playing hide-and-seek. This is also a great game for kids and dogs to play together.

Begin by holding your dog; this will make him want to follow the person who hides. Eventually you can teach him to sit and stay or wait next to you until the other player hides and then calls him.

When your dog finds this person, she celebrates with your dog. Your dog can have fun, receive treats, and play tug-of-war. When this person is done rewarding your dog, she holds him and gives you a verbal signal to let you know that it is your turn. Hide and call your dog with your signal. When he finds you, celebrate. It is up to you how you reward your dog. Do something that he enjoys.

When your dog understands that the object of the game is to find the caller, you can increase the distance between players and make your hiding places more challenging.

Three-or-More-People Games

If there are more than two people in your family, you can add a third player to the Basic Two-Person Recall game and the Hide-and-Seek game. These games are helpful if your dog needs to learn to come to different people.

Follow the instructions for the Basic Two-Person Recall and Hide-and-Seek games, but add an extra player or players. Be sure that all new people play the Basic One-Person Recall game first with your dog, so he is accustomed to coming to each of you before he starts playing the game with multiple players. For the Basic Two-Person Recall game all players should begin the game close enough to each other that they can use their hand signal or lure your dog to them if necessary. For the Hide-and-Seek game, players should not hide from your dog at first but should position themselves so that your dog can see them. Once your dog understands the game, players can make their hiding places a little more challenging for him. Remember to add a second verbal signal (such as "Great job" or "Okay") after your dog has finished his treat or been rewarded to let other players know when it is their turn to call him.

Always end games on a successful note.

Teaching Your Dog to Listen to a Verbal Signal

The Basic One-Person and Two-Person Recall games and Hide-and-Seek teach your dog a pattern of behavior. The one-person games teach him to get a treat or an object and then return to you for more. The two-person games teach him to run back and forth between people to get rewards. After teaching him these patterns, you can add a word or signal meaning "Come," and he will associate this signal with coming to you. Since dogs love patterns, many dogs simply follow the rules of the game without listening to your "Come" signal. This game teaches your dog to *listen* for your verbal signal before coming to you. Some dogs are naturally very good at this. Others need to improve their listening skills.

Call your dog using your verbal "Come" signal. When he gets to you, give him a treat. Praise him after you give him the treat. The other person playing then calls him. When your dog comes to that person, she delivers praise and a treat. If your dog races to you or the other player before either of you have used your verbal signal, do not give him a treat. If your dog happens to run to you before you call him, the other player can call him again and then reward him when he comes to her. The objective is to reward him for listening to the verbal signal.

Increase the distance between players as your dog gets better at playing the game. Be sure to add a second verbal signal (such as "Good Job" or "Perfect") after your dog has finished his treat to let other players know when it is their turn to call him.

Playing a Recall Game While You Distract Your Dog

Two people are needed for this game. One person intentionally distracts your dog. You are the caller, and you do not have any toys or treats; the person who distracts your dog should have all the goodies but should not give him any treats or toys.

Call your dog with your designated signal. The person you are playing with tries to mildly distract your dog. Since your dog is being distracted, he will likely ignore you. Keep calling, using prompts and whistling, or run in the opposite direction; do anything that you can think of to get your dog to approach you. If your dog comes to you, the person who has the treats or toys either runs over and gives your dog a treat or tosses a toy to you so that you can play with your dog. By running up to you to give your dog a treat, the treat-bearer distracts your dog again and draws him away from you, and you can call your dog to come to you once more. When your dog comes to you, the other person once again runs to deliver a treat or gives you a toy so that you can play with him. Your dog will learn that the only way to get a reward is to listen to you — the caller — and to leave the person who is distracting him. Always praise your dog and give him better rewards for recalls in the face of distractions. You can vary the rules of this game as you and your dog get better at playing it.

When your dog gets good at this game, you can make it more

advanced by giving him treats only when he responds to your verbal signal. At this stage, if your dog rushes over to you before being called (again, dogs catch on to patterns quickly), *don't* give him a treat. The object of the game is for your dog not to just come to you but to come to you specifically when you call him.

Do not move on to new games too quickly. If you keep adding new rules and standards for your dog to follow before he has learned the basics, he will soon become confused, get frustrated, and stop playing with you.

You can vary this game by playing a two-person recall game with a person your dog least attends to. When your dog comes to the caller, the caller praises him and gives lots of fantastic rewards. The person whom your dog is most responsive to also rewards him for listening to the caller.

Target Game

This game is for dogs who are not very toy motivated or who don't know how to play, such as many abused or rescued dogs. If your dog is clicker trained (see the next paragraph), he will learn this game rather quickly. If your dog is sound sensitive, you can condition him to another noise or verbal marker, such as "Yes," "Good," "Nice," or "Great." Every time your dog nudges the toy with his muzzle or touches it, praise your dog with your verbal marker, and reward him with food.

A clicker is a little box, plastic or metal, that makes a clicking sound. Clickers are available online and from many pet supply stores. A clicker-trained dog is one who associates the clicking sound with a food reward. The clicker is a *positive* marker for your dog. It marks a behavior that you want or like. The food reward then follows, and your dog learns that he performed the behavior you wanted.

Start with a toy, a ball, or an object your dog likes. Show him the toy. When he touches it with either his nose or his paws, click the clicker, or praise him with your verbal marker, and give him a treat.

Increase the distance between you and the toy. Your dog should go to the toy, touch it, and then come back to you for a food reward. Click the clicker, or praise him, as he touches the toy. Then call him back to you with your designated "Come" signal. The object of the game is for your dog to touch the ball or toy and come back to you for a treat. The game will look like fetch, except that your dog will not bring the toy back to you. Instead, you will have to get the toy and toss it so that he can run to it, touch it with his nose or paw, and then run back to you for a reward.

SUMMARY

Release Word, Attention, and Recall

- Teach your dog a release word. A release word indicates to your dog that there is a transition and that he no longer has to engage in the behavior you were requesting of him. "Okay," "No more," or "All done" are examples of release words.
- Always use your dog's name positively.
- Change the inflection in your voice and use high-pitched noises to get a dog's attention.
- Make calling your dog's name relevant to him. When he hears his name, something should happen that relates to him.
- Don't use your dog's name if you are going to do something that he dislikes.
- Your dog's name does not mean "No" or "Come."

- Don't chase your dog if you want him to come to you; if you want him to approach you, run or walk in the opposite direction instead.
- Always reward your dog when he comes after you call him.
- Don't punish your dog or do something that he dislikes after he comes to you.
- Sometimes you may need to get your dog. Don't call him to come to you while you are trying to catch him.
- By playing recall games, you can teach your dog the meaning of your recall signal and make coming to you an enjoyable experience for him.

TEACHING SIT, STAND, AND LIE DOWN

"Sit," "Stand," and "Down" are verbal signals that indicate body positions. In the stand position your dog is standing on all fours. When your dog lies down, he is in the down position. There are two down positions: a posed down and a relaxed down. A posed down is the position in which your dog looks like a sphinx (his body weight is evenly distributed over his back legs). A relaxed down is the position in which he is leaning in one direction or is favoring one hip over the other.

You must teach your dog two sitting positions: sitting in front of you and sitting next to you. Picture yourself on a walk with your dog. When you meet someone, you may want your dog to sit next to you. Keep in mind that dogs learn exactly what you teach them. If you always teach your dog to sit in front of you, he will always face you when he sits. If you then ask him to sit next to you, he will pivot to sit in front of you. This can be problematic for people who want to teach their dogs to sit next to them before crossing the street. They stop at a curb and ask their dogs to sit;

their dogs comply by walking partially into the road to sit in front of them.

It is also important to teach your dog to sit or lie down in many locations — especially in the specific locations and situations in which you would like him to perform these behaviors. Teach your dog to sit and lie down in the car. In addition, teach him to sit or lie down for nonfood rewards. These might include opening doors for him (including car doors, if he likes car rides), taking him off the leash, letting him run and play with other dogs, and petting him.

If your dog is older or seems reluctant to sit, he may be having trouble with his hips, knees, or joints. Ask for another behavior that is easy for him to do instead, such as looking at you or waiting. (If your dog seems particularly hesitant or uncomfortable, seek veterinary attention.)

Sit

Hold a piece of food in front of your dog's nose. He may nibble or lick your hand. This is okay. Imagine a half-inch length of string running between his nose and your hand. Lift your hand slightly, making a little arc from the bottom of your dog's chin to the top of his forehead. He should sit by following your hand. Be careful not to hold the treat too high, or he will just jump or stare at you. If he seems to be moving around a lot, more than likely your hand is moving around a lot. Keep your hand steady. When he lifts his head up, his rear should naturally hit the floor. The moment your dog sits, praise him and give him the treat.

When your dog begins to anticipate your hand motion, wean him off seeing the treat. Keep your hand flat while holding the treat under your thumb or between your fingers with your palm facing up. Make an upward motion with your hand. When your dog sits, give him the treat. When you can use a flat hand to instruct him to sit, start delivering treats with your other hand. You are now using a hand signal. Reward your dog profusely for sitting without being lured by food.

FIGURE 19.
Sit signal.

The next step is to put the food in your pocket. Show your dog your empty hands. Ask him to sit by using your hand signal. He may hesitate. Wait. When he sits, praise him and give him a handful of treats. Say "Sit" when you know he will sit with your hand signal. By pairing the verbal signal with your dog's behavior, you are teaching him the meaning of your hand signal. Always keep training sessions short and sweet. End on a good note.

Stand

When your dog is sitting, hold a treat in front of his nose with the palm of your hand facing him. Pull your arm back in one straight motion to the side of your leg or in front of your leg as you take a step back. Your dog will stand to follow the food. Immediately give him the treat. You can then lure him back to a sitting position by moving your hand slightly over his head. When he sits, give him a treat. Keep repeating this by rewarding your dog for each position change. When he catches on, hide the food in your hand by placing the treat under your thumb or between your fingers, and use a flat hand to signal him. When making a formal hand signal, remember to deliver treats from your other hand. Add a verbal cue, such as "Stand," when you know your dog will stand on seeing your hand signal.

FIGURE 20. Bringing Lucy to a standing position.

Sit from the Side

With your dog standing next to you, position him between you and a barrier such as a wall, sofa, chair, or tree. Have your dog stand next to you, between you and the barrier. Put food in front of his nose and lure him into a sitting position by making a little arc from the bottom of his chin to the top of his head. By positioning him between you and a wall or another barrier, you can prevent him from rotating to sit in front of you. Lure your dog to stand, then sit, then stand again. Reward him for each position change. Keep your arm close to your body when luring him to sit next to you. If your hand is too far in front of you, he will sit in front of you, not next to you. Once your hand motion is enough to signal him to sit, wean him off the food lure. Hide the food when you signal him. Add your verbal cue when you know he will sit on seeing your hand signal. Reward him for sitting next to you.

FIGURE 21. Teaching sit from the side.

Lie Down

It is easier to teach your dog to lie down when he is already sitting. Have patience if you have a little dog or a dog with very long or very short legs. It can be challenging for some dogs initially to understand what you want from them. Once your dog understands you, he should have little difficulty lying down on cue.

Position your dog on a comfortable surface, such as a rug or a dog bed (with little dogs, you can practice on a bed or a sofa). Start with your dog in a sitting position. Hold a food treat in your hand (between your fingers or under your thumb), and put that hand under your dog's nose with your palm facing the floor. Bring your hand gently down to the floor. Your dog may lick or paw at your hand or get confused and lick your face for a moment. Wait patiently. The instant he lies down, give him a handful of treats or a particularly desirable treat. Bring him out of the down position by luring him to stand or sit. Alternate luring him to sit and lie down. You can also lure him to stand, ask him to sit, and then lure him to lie down again. Add the cue "Down" or "Lie Down" when you know that he will lie down with the lure or by following your hand motion.

When your dog seems very comfortable with lying down when he sees your hand motioning to the floor, exaggerate your hand motion. Keep your hand flat, palm facing down, and bring your hand to the floor. Treat your dog with your other hand (as you did when teaching your dog to sit for you). You are now rewarding your dog for following your hand signal and not the lure.

You can shape lying down for dogs who have difficulty. Place your dog on a soft comfortable surface, such as a rug or dog bed. Ask him to sit. Hold a piece of food in front of his nose and bring your hand gently to the floor. Give your dog treats continually as he follows your hand. Stop giving him treats if he stands or sits up again. Eventually he will lie down all the way. Be patient. Shaping a down may take a few practice sessions. Give your dog a handful of treats when he finally lies down. Always keep training sessions short and sweet.

FIGURE 22. Lucy lies down by following my hand signal.

Relaxed Down

If your dog lies down in a posed position, he may immediately pop up into a standing or sitting position after you give him a treat. To prevent this, you can teach him to lie down in a relaxed way.

A relaxed down is generally more stable than a posed down and is more conducive to teaching a reliable "stay," "relax," or "settle." Many dogs will naturally position themselves so that they lean in one direction or favor one hip over the other. Some dogs may lie down with their back legs outstretched behind them.

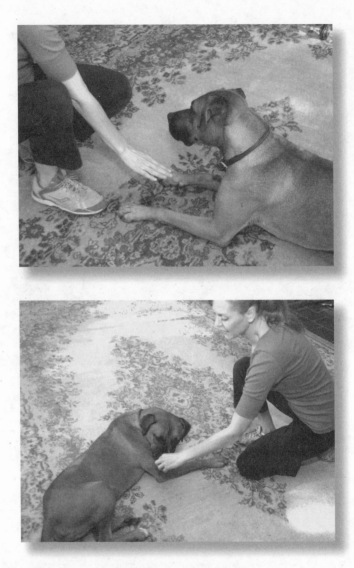

FIGURES 23 and 24. Teaching a relaxed down.

Lure your dog into the down position. He will lie down so that his weight is equally distributed on both hips. Keep your hands low to the ground as you treat him. Take the treat you used to lure him and run your hand holding the treat very slowly up one of his forelegs. If he seems to be leaning toward his left hip, choose his right foreleg. If he seems to be leaning toward his right hip, choose his left foreleg. Start close to his paw and run your hand along his leg, over his elbow toward his shoulder. He will lick your hand and nudge it with his nose. Keep your hand close to his body as he nudges you. As he sniffs and nudges your hand, he will shift his body weight to the opposite hip. When he does this, reward him. Stand up and repeat the exercise.

When he shifts his body weight after you lure him, hide the food so that your hand motion or touch on his shoulder signals him to shift position. Reward him profusely for shifting his body weight to one hip.

SUMMARY

Sit, Stand, and Down

- Teach your dog to sit next to you and in front of you.
- Teach your dog to sit and lie down in different locations.
- When teaching your dog to lie down, provide a soft surface for him such as a rug, carpet, or dog bed. You can shape lying down for dogs who have difficulty.
- There are two down positions: a posed down and a relaxed down. A relaxed down is more conducive to teaching a reliable stay.
- Wean your dog off the food lure by hiding it from him. You can do this by placing food under your thumb or between your fingers while you lure him into position.
- Turn the hand motion you use to lure your dog into a hand signal.

- When your dog regularly follows your hand signal, give him treats with your other hand.
- Add your verbal cue when you know that you can signal your dog to sit or lie down.
- Replace food rewards with nonfood rewards, such as opening doors, putting on or taking off the leash, or throwing toys for your dog to chase.

TEACHING LEAVE IT, THANK YOU, AND DROP OR GIVE

As discussed earlier, dogs have a simple notion of ownership. In dog culture, if an object is in your paws or in your mouth, it's yours. If no one possesses an object, ownership is determined by who is closest to that object or who gets to it first. Many misunderstandings take place between people and dogs when it comes to property and ownership. From a dog's perspective, if you aren't holding, working with, or eating an object, it's not yours.

This causes confusion for dogs. We frequently reprimand dogs for stealing socks, wallets, pillows, stuffed animals, tissue or toilet paper, remote controls, or food left out on the table. We try to take these items away from dogs and then wonder why the dogs avoid us, growl, or clamp their jaws down on the object so that we can't pry it out of their mouths.

Dogs tend not to take things directly from each other's mouths. In dog culture it is considered rude. But people constantly take things from dogs' mouths and assume that the dogs know that these items belong to us. From your dog's point of view, an item on the floor or on the sidewalk is not yours to tell him to leave alone. Likewise, if he picks up an object and you try to take it out of his mouth, he will resist you because you have no right to take it. If an item is of high value to your dog, he may growl at you when you approach him. In his view, you have no right to it — unless, of course, he *wants* to give it to you.

The more your dog values an item, the more difficult it will be for him to give it to you. If you punish or reprimand him for taking an object, he will grow afraid of you, and any of several things may happen: He may try to scarf down the object when you are not looking (common sense on his part); he may see you coming and gobble the item down quickly; he may growl at you for your rude behavior to tell you to back off; or he may run away from you. The best way to teach your dog to abandon an object or give it to you is by teaching him that it's rewarding to do so. Dogs do not want to give away what rightfully belongs to them. However, you can teach your dog to feel good about giving you his belongings.

Leave It

The beginning stage of this exercise teaches your dog to back away from an object you have in your hands. Once he understands your cue to "Leave it," you can make this exercise more challenging by holding more valuable items or by lowering your hand to the ground. Ultimately he will leave the items on the floor. This exercise is messy at first, but dogs love it and learn it quickly.

Hold a food treat in your hand and make a fist. Present your fist to your dog and allow him to lick and paw at your hand. Do not pull your hand away from him, or you will encourage him to follow it. Don't say anything. You are teaching him to "Leave it" passively. Your dog will learn that he gets what he wants when he does what you want him to, which is to not lick or paw at your hand. Give him the treat the moment he stops nudging or pawing at you. He might only be getting ready to nudge or paw at you again, but through repetition and good timing on your part he will realize that he gets the food by moving his nose *away* from your hand. After a series of repetitions, your dog should back away from your hand or simply watch it politely when you present the treat. Once he no longer nudges or paws you, say "Leave it" in a nice tone of voice as you show him your fist. Praise and reward him when he backs away from the treat. By pairing the words "Leave it" with your dog's behavior you are teaching him the meaning of the verbal cue. If your dog still nudges your fist with his nose when you present the treat, do not add your verbal cue. Wait until he is demonstrating the behavior that you want before you start labeling it verbally.

FIGURES 25 and 26. "Leave it" exercises.

Once your dog starts backing away from your fist and responding to your cue to "Leave it," make the exercise a little more challenging by holding the food under your thumb in an open palm. Position your hand next to your dog's face but not under his nose or chin. (If you hold the food under his nose, he will think you are offering him the treat because this is how you position your hand when you are feeding him.) Your dog will probably lick or paw at your hand again. When he backs away or stops licking or pawing at you, praise him and give him the treat. Say "Leave it" when he leaves the food that you present to him.

Once your dog understands that he needs to back away from your hand, you can start to increase the amount of time that he has to wait. Ask him to "Leave it" for a few seconds longer with each presentation. If he starts to nudge you again, you may be waiting too long. You want your dog to succeed. Continue this exercise until he leaves the food in your open hand with every presentation. Then start rewarding him with treats from your other hand (the hand not presenting the food). Your dog is now being rewarded for completely leaving the food presented in your hand.

Always give your dog more treats or a better treat than the one he is leaving in your hand. To increase the difficulty of this exercise, gradually lower your hand to the floor. Then place the food treat on the floor. Once the food is on the floor, lure him away from the food with another treat. Say "Leave it" when he leaves the treat on the ground. Reward him for not touching the treat or for backing away from it. If you see him going for the treat, cover it with your hand. When he backs away from the treat say "Leave it," pause, pick up the treat from the floor, and reward him. Don't go too fast or try to make this exercise too difficult at first. Set your dog up for success.

FIGURES 27 and 28. "Leave it" exercises.

Please don't reprimand your dog when he touches or paws at your hand. He will not automatically understand what you want. Give him a bunch of treats or some very good treats for especially good behaviors. It is easier to start by giving him treats with the same hand that is holding the food. Once you are comfortable holding the food under your thumb or in your open palm, begin giving your dog treats with your other hand. You are now rewarding him for leaving the food in your hand entirely alone.

When outside on walks, carry especially good treats with you. When you see something on the ground your dog may want to put in his mouth, make a distracting noise, such as "Ah-Ah" or "Hey," and lure him away from the item with a food treat. Say "Leave it" as he leaves or ignores the item on the ground. Make sure to remove the item you don't want your dog to have or guide him away from it by luring him to follow you or by redirecting him to another activity. Reward him heavily for leaving items outside. He will soon happily listen to your "Ah-Ah" and "Leave it" prompts.

Note: Instead of using a "Leave it" cue, you can signal your dog for eye contact when he passes something on the ground you don't want him to have, such as that moldy pizza crust or fast-food wrapper. He will be less inclined to grab an item from the ground if he is being praised and rewarded for looking at you instead.

Thank You

"Thank you" is what you say when you take away an object that your dog already has. Start with items that are of little value to your dog or that you don't mind him having. Toys, sticks, and balls are good objects to start with. When your dog has or plays with one of these items, put a treat in front of his nose. He should look expectantly at you for the treat. Extend your hand and say, "Thank you," as you take the item from him, give him the treat, and then give him back the item. He may follow you for more treats, but don't give them to him. Only give him treats when you take something from him, and always give him something better than the object that you have taken away. Then give him back the object he originally had. Once he begins to release or offer his objects to you, phase out the food lure by hiding the treat in your hand or putting it in your pocket. Extend your hand, say, "Thank you," and take the object. Give him abundant goodies and remember to give the object back to him. Eventually you will be able to take something from your dog even if you are not going to return it. "Thank you" is a great exercise to teach puppies.

Drop or Give

When your dog is carrying something in his mouth, you may want him to give the object to you without your having to take it from him. This is a "Drop" or "Give" command. There are many ways to teach this behavior. All are rewarding for your dog. Below are some enjoyable games to play with your dog that can teach him to drop or give an item to you.

Drop or Give Games

Drop Toys

If your dog is toy motivated, start with two or three toys of equal value. Ball-motivated dogs love this game. Entice your dog with a toy by playing with it. When your dog shows interest, toss it up for him or bounce it on the ground for him to catch. Don't throw or toss the toy far away from you. When your dog takes the toy in his mouth, play with the other toys you have in your hand. Your dog will soon lose interest in the toy he is carrying and will drop it. When he does, praise him and toss one of the toys you have or bounce another ball on the ground. Pick up the toy he dropped and repeat the game. Say "Drop" or "Give" every time he drops the ball or toy. You are teaching him the meaning of the word by pairing it with his behavior. When he drops the toy or ball, reward him with one of the other toys or balls you have. Your dog will soon find dropping toys and balls fun, and will begin to do it on cue, especially if you reward him for it!

Drop or Give for a Treat

This exercise is very similar to teaching "Thank you," only you do not take the item from your dog. Instead, you wait for him to drop the object for you. You then reward him and give the object back to him. Wait for your dog to carry an item you don't mind him having. When he is carrying the object in his mouth, hold a treat close to his nose. Wait for him to drop the item. He will naturally do so because he wants the treat. When he drops or releases the item, say "Drop" or "Give." Pick up the object or item he dropped, praise him, and give him a really good food reward. Then give him back his item. After a few repetitions, when you say "Drop" or "Give," your dog should drop the object for you. Praise and reward him generously when he does.

SUMMARY

Leave It, Thank You, and Drop or Give

- Dogs have a simple notion of ownership. If no one is eating, touching, or directly holding an object, ownership is determined by who is closest to the object or who gets to it first.
- The more valuable an item is to your dog, the more difficult it will be for him to relinquish it.
- Dogs tend not to remove things directly from each other's mouths.

- Punishing your dog for taking an item will make him afraid of you and will either cause him to run away from you with the object or encourage him to take things when you aren't looking.
- When teaching your dog to give things to you, take an object away from him, give him a special food treat, and then give him back the object.
- The best way to teach your dog to leave an object or give it to you is by teaching him that it is rewarding to do so.

Wait and Stay

The difference between waiting and staying is that waiting is usually a short-term behavior that provides your dog with something he wants after he waits for it. He may wait for you to open the door for him, to put on or take off his leash, to cross the street, or for you to throw a ball or toy for him. Waiting simply means that your dog does not move forward.

Staying (or "settling" or "relaxing") is a longer-term behavior. There is not necessarily a reward at the end of staying. The reward is staying in and of itself. Your dog may stay as you eat dinner or settle comfortably on his mat while you have guests over. He may be asked to stay or settle in the car. As he stays, he gets rewarded. You may choose to say "Relax" when your dog lies down comfortably in a relaxed down position and then "Settle" for your stay command. The words you choose are not particularly important. What is important is that you are consistent, know what you are teaching, and have realistic expectations for your dog so that he can succeed.

Teaching a dog to stay happens gradually. When you give your dog positive reinforcement for sitting, standing, or lying down for a specified amount of time, during distractions, and as you walk away from him, you are teaching him to stay. You must first teach him to sit, stand, or lie down on cue in the settings you want him to stay before you begin stay training.

Begin by teaching your dog to sit, stand, or lie down for a specified length of time. Start with a few seconds. Once he can reliably stay in a sit, stand, or down position for a certain length of time (say, thirty to sixty seconds), you can then put distance between you and your dog — or you can stand next to him and add mild distractions. As always, set him up for success. Praise and reward him as he stays. Start with short intervals, and don't ask him to stay for too long or increase the distance between the two of you too quickly.

You must also teach your dog a release word: a word that tells him that you expect nothing more of him and that he is free to do as he pleases. By teaching him a release word, you will avoid teaching him that the food reward you give him means that he no longer needs to engage in the behavior that you are asking for. If you don't teach him a release word, the food will become the end goal and will no longer work to reinforce a behavior. Over time, this becomes bribery. This can cause a jack-in-the-box response. A dog lies down, is given a treat, and then he pops back up again. By teaching your dog a release word, he will learn that treats do not mean that he is finished performing a behavior but that he is doing a terrific job at that behavior. If you do not teach him a release word he will have no way of knowing how long you would like him to stay for. He will become confused, and his behavior will become unreliable. Make it clear when you want your dog to perform a behavior and when he is free to do as he likes.

Ask your dog to sit or lie down. Do not reward him. If he does not know how to sit or lie down on cue, you are not ready to teach him to stay. Say "Stay," show your dog a hand signal (palm facing him, fingers toward the sky or ceiling), and give him treats. Then say your release word (such as "Free," "Okay," or "Finished") and stop giving him treats. Walk away from him or turn your back on him. He will probably get up and walk around or follow you. This is fine. A few minutes later, ask him to sit or lie down again. Again, say "Stay," show him your hand signal, and give him treats intermittently the entire time that he remains in the position you asked for. Say your release word and stop giving him treats. Increase the time interval between giving treats to your dog as he gets better at lying down or sitting for extended periods of time. Stop giving him treats after you release him.

If your dog breaks the stay, immediately get him back into a sit or down position and start over. If you find yourself frequently starting over, decrease the amount of time that you ask him to sit or lie down for or limit the distractions around him.

When you first start adding distractions to the exercise, stand next to your dog. Reward him with treats during and immediately following a distraction. Eventually you will deliver treats only after the distraction has passed. Then you can release him. Remember to use better rewards and decrease the amount of time that you expect him to stay for when you increase the distance between you and your dog or add distractions.

To teach your dog to stay when you are at a distance from him, think of yourself as a bungee cord. Ask him to sit or lie down. Tell him to "Stay," and take a step away from him. If he stays, step back to him and give him a treat. Repeat this several times, and then release him.

FIGURE 29. Teaching Jake to stay from the front at a distance.

FIGURE 30. Teaching Sebby to stay with my back turned to him.

Body-Blocking

You can teach a dog to wait, and correct a break of a stay, by body-blocking him. Remember that face-forward body language is mildly threatening. You can use body-blocking as a way to take up space, such as a doorway or counter, to claim it as your own. This prevents a dog from moving beyond the boundary you have established. If you face your dog directly and walk toward him, you may notice that he moves or walks away from you, out of your personal space. You can use this approach to keep him back from a doorway or to back him away from a counter he is obsessing about. Instead of grabbing him by the collar or yelling at him, get in front of him, face him directly, and slowly walk forward in his direction. If he tries to move around you, block him. When he has moved back a few steps, pause and stand still for about two seconds. Be very calm. When he waits, say "Stay" or "Wait" so that he associates the word with the behavior of waiting, praise him, and continue to do what you were previously doing (that is, begin to open the door or go back to the counter). Go back to him and reward him generously for waiting.

Remember, dogs are context or situational learners. If you teach him to wait in the hallway as you open the door for guests to enter, he will apply that behavior to that doorway. If you want him to wait while you open the car door, you must teach him to wait in that context.

DISTANCE TRAINING

It is not terribly difficult to teach your dog to respond to requests from a distance. Start with an exercise you have already taught him. Stand very close to him when you begin the exercise. When he performs the desired behavior reliably, take a step back. You can tether him, ask him to stay, or keep him behind a baby gate to keep him from following you as you back away. Don't increase the distance between the two of you too quickly or you may confuse him. If your dog seems perplexed or doesn't perform the behavior you ask for, step closer to him and ask him again. When he performs the behavior, reward him profusely. When you step away from him again and ask him to perform a desired behavior, he will anticipate that you will return to him to give him a reward.

Another person can also give your dog treats for following your requests. This person should remain next to your dog at all times so that she can give him treats. Your dog can be on a leash to keep him from following you as you back away. You should not have any treats on you. Begin by standing next to your dog, and ask him to perform a behavior. When he complies, the person helping you gives him a treat. Gradually increase the distance between you and your dog. The person giving him treats should give him better or more treats when your dog responds to your requests from farther away.

The Crazy Human and Dog Game

This is a great game to teach your dog because it reinforces all the behaviors you've already taught him and teaches him to listen to you even when he is excited. The object of the game is to reward your dog with play for listening to your instructions.

You can be creative when playing this game. Ask your dog to perform one or two behaviors. When he performs a behavior you ask for, celebrate by acting goofy, running, throwing a toy for him to chase, feeding him yummy treats, letting him give you kisses, or playing tug-of-war. Be happy! Your dog will see that you are having a good time. Get him excited, and then ask him to sit or to leave an object alone or to lie down and stay. Pause. Once he performs the behavior, release him and celebrate again. The reward is play — food doesn't need to be part of this game. Play the game for short periods when your dog is bored or antsy or needs exercise.

SUMMARY

Wait, Stay, and Distance Training

- The difference between waiting and staying is that waiting is usually a short-term behavior that provides your dog with something he wants after he waits for it. Staying (or "settling" or "relaxing") is a longer-term behavior. He may stay as you eat dinner or settle comfortably on his mat while you have guests over.
- Teaching your dog to stay happens gradually
- Teach your dog to stay while you're at different angles to him, including having your back to him.
- Teach your dog to sit or lie down in the settings where you want him to stay before you begin teaching him to stay in those settings.
- Reward your dog for staying — not for breaking the stay.
- If your dog breaks a stay, first ask him to sit or lie down again before giving the instruction to stay. If he continues to break position, decrease the amount of time you ask him to stay for. You may also need to limit the distractions around him.
- Teach your dog a release word so that he knows when he is no longer expected to perform a behavior.
- You can teach your dog to wait, or correct a break of a stay, by body-blocking him. Body-blocking is a way for you to take up space, such as a doorway or counter, to

claim it as your own. It prevents your dog from moving forward beyond the boundary you have established.

- Teach your dog to wait or stay in the settings or contexts in which you would like him to stay.

- To teach your dog an instruction at a distance, ask him to stay, leash him, keep him behind a baby gate, or have a friend stand next to him and give him treats. Stand next to your dog at first. Ask him to perform a behavior. Reward him when he performs it, and then step away from him. Ask him to perform the behavior again. When he complies, return to him to reward him or have your friend give him a treat.

- Exaggerate your hand motions and speak louder when signaling to your dog from a distance.

- Reinforce all the behaviors that you teach your dog by playing the Crazy Human and Dog game. You can both have fun and act silly while your dog learns to listen to you.

Chapter Four

JUMPING, CHEWING, BARKING, HOUSETRAINING, AND STOOL-EATING

CALMING BODY LANGUAGE

Humans tend to use intense body language when interacting with other animals. As primates, we reach in front of us to grab and touch objects, and we face individuals directly. Direct frontal body language can frighten and inhibit many dogs. It can also intensify anxiety and aggression, increase mouthiness, and cause a dog to jump on you. By being cognizant of your body language and modifying it around dogs, you can help them be more relaxed and comfortable with you.

Angle yourself slightly when interacting with dogs, as opposed to facing them directly or leaning over them. Stand or kneel next to or parallel to them, or at a perpendicular angle to them. Pet your dog under his chin and on his chest. Try not to face him directly as you pet him or to pet him on his head.

When he approaches, sniffs, or kisses you, avert your gaze slightly for a moment. Your dog will find this a friendly gesture. If he gets too excited around you, turn your back on him and cease all eye contact. Only pay attention to him when he calms down.

FIGURE 31. Petting Kiva on her chest. My hand remains under her head.

FIGURE 32. Angling my body away from Lucy slightly, as I pet her under her chin.

PREVENTING AND RESOLVING JUMPING

Memorize this statement: "Life happens on all fours." Give your dog all the attention he desires and deserves, but only do so when he has all four paws on the ground. Try to catch and reward these behaviors (such as standing, sitting, and lying down) *before* your dog feels it is in his best interests to jump. If he needs to show you that he is sitting by jumping on you first to get your attention, you will end up reinforcing jumping — not sitting.

If your dog jumps on you, pivot away from him and end all eye contact. You may have to do this a few times before he calms down. When he is on all fours again, give him attention, eye contact, or whatever else he was wanting. If you have something that your dog wants, and he jumps on you, remove the item or turn away from him. When he is on all fours again, offer him the item.

FIGURE 33. Turning my back to Kiva when she jumps.

Use this same approach when sitting on sofas or chairs. The instant your dog jumps on you, end eye contact and pivot your legs away from him. Give him attention when he is back on all fours. *Do not give him attention too quickly after he jumps.* Wait at least three to five seconds before you interact with him again. If he climbs all over you while you are seated, stand up and turn your back to him. Withdraw your attention until he calms down.

Tips for Discouraging Jumping Up on Guests and for Meeting People Outside

In entryways: Direct your dog to an activity away from the door. Teach him to wait or stay at the doorway when guests enter, or call him to you whenever a person enters and have him sit or lie down for food treats. Play with him with toys from a toy bin whenever someone enters the house. Teach him to fetch or play tug with a toy. Give him something to chew on or carry. Dogs tend not to jump when they are carrying objects in their mouths. Visitors should remain calm and not give your dog too much attention immediately on entering. Likewise, stay relaxed when you open the door and greet guests.

FIGURE 34. Andy, Lucy, and Sebby learn to stay back from the doorway when guests enter. Athena the kitty watches.

Outside: When introducing your dog to a new person, kneel down next to him to keep him from jumping up. This will also encourage other people to stand next to him or to approach him from the side. Give your dog treats while someone new is petting him on the head. When the new person stops petting your dog, stop giving him treats. Your dog is less likely to jump while he is eating and may come to enjoy being petted on the head.

If your dog really likes people, you can teach him that whenever he meets a new person, if he remains calm he will get attention and be petted. You can also give him treats for sitting when a person approaches. If your dog jumps or stands up, the person can walk away from him, or you can stop giving your dog treats. You can practice this exercise with a friend. Eventually your friend should be able to approach your dog and pet him while your dog remains calm and sits.

Teach your dog to walk with you and to look at you when people pass by. Give him treats when a person passes by, and stop treating him when the person walks away or has gone. This is a good technique to use if your dog is shy. It reinforces your dog for looking at you, and it makes having people pass by a pleasurable experience for him. It is also a nice approach to use if your dog is easily distracted.

While talking to a stranger, reward your dog for standing, sitting, or lying down. You do not necessarily need to instruct him to sit, stand, or lie down; just give him treats whenever he exhibits these behaviors, and he will perform them more often.

CHEWING AND PLAY-BITING

All puppies and young dogs mouth objects and play-bite in order to explore their environment. Just as human toddlers explore the environment by touching and tasting, puppies and young dogs want to chew the world — or at least try to taste it. When puppies and dogs are overly tired they may also act out. If you find that your dog is out of control and none of the methods discussed below seems to help, he may just need a good nap.

Prevention is the best way to deal with chewing and play-biting. Give your dog a toy bin filled with fun toys. Keep food-dispensing toys in a separate location. Always play with your dog with toys from the bin and keep the bin in an accessible location. Reward and praise your dog for getting toys from the toy bin. When your dog is done playing with his toys, put them back into the bin. Do not leave the toys on the floor, or they will lose value for your dog.

FIGURE 35. Lucy chooses a toy from the toy bin.

To prevent chewing, mist items that you do not want damaged with all-natural concentrated orange-citrus spray. Most dogs do not like the smell of citrus and will avoid objects that have been sprayed. *Never use synthetic chemical sprays.*

The following exercises should help to eliminate play-biting and will teach your dog to bite or mouth you softly. If you try to eliminate play-biting too soon — especially in young puppies — two things may happen: One, you fail miserably and unintentionally encourage your dog to mouth or bite you harder. Two, you succeed and your dog never learns to control how hard he bites.

Dogs who live in groups have good mouth control. They play-bite, give each other kisses, and gnaw on bones by varying the amount of pressure they exert with their mouths and jaws. Mouth control is a learned behavior. A young puppy develops it by playing with other dogs. When dogs play, if one dog bites too hard, the dog who gets bitten yelps or cries out and immediately stops playing.

Your puppy will instinctively learn to inhibit his bite if you make a high-pitched yelp and stop playing and interacting with him the instant he bites or mouths you too hard. If you try to reprimand or punish him by yelling at him, grabbing his muzzle, or pinning him to the ground, you will just get him more excited and encourage him to continue to attack you or frighten him so badly that he doesn't want to play with you anymore. Neither method will teach him mouth control.

Teaching Dogs to Soften Their Mouths and Eliminate Play-Biting

If your dog bites really hard during play, begin this exercise when his bite hurts you or when you can feel his teeth. If your dog is older but still bites hard, begin this exercise as soon as you feel pressure. When it seems as if your dog is becoming sensitive to how hard he is biting you, you can implement this exercise when he mouths you or bites you softly, even when it doesn't hurt. Teach your dog that humans are wimps when it comes to being bitten.

When your dog bites you, quickly make a high-pitched noise to startle him. This "Ouch" cue should sound like a yelp — not a scolding or a punishment. But don't keep whimpering; your dog will just think that you're weird. As soon as he bites you, make your yelping noise and look away from him. If your dog looks startled or perplexed and tries to solicit your attention, ignore him for about twenty seconds. You are giving him a time-out for hurting you. Do not interact with him in any way. Do not say "No." Do not take him into another room. This teaches him that it hurts you when he bites you, and if he bites you, you won't play with him anymore. He should be able to associate your "Ouch" cue with the bite. Timing is important. If you yelp when he hasn't bitten you, he won't understand why you are telling him that you're hurt.

After about twenty seconds, play with your dog again. You want to let him know that even though you like him and want to play, you don't like it when he bites you. If he mouths or bites you softly, you may allow it. You can always redirect the behavior and encourage your dog to play with a toy. After a time-out, if your dog continues to bite you and it hurts, yelp the instant he bites and ignore him again. Do not make eye contact with him. This time ignore him for about forty seconds. Under no circumstances should you interact with him.

After the second time-out, play with your dog again. Encourage him to play with his toys, or pet him gently while sitting next to him. If he bites you again, yelp or give your "Ouch" cue, and leave the room. Do not bring him with you, and be sure that he can't follow you. It is more effective if you leave him alone for the time-out. After about sixty seconds, return to the room and play with him again. Always encourage him to play with his toys.

If your dog bites your clothing or legs as you walk, freeze. Most puppies grow out of this. If you react, you will encourage him to keep attacking you. Be boring. Don't move. If your dog is obsessed with your clothing or with biting your legs, mist a little citrus spray on your clothing. This should keep him from wanting to bite your clothes. Only yelp or make an "Ouch" noise when he bites your skin. If you need to physically remove him from your pant leg, be calm and avoid making eye contact with him while doing so. Again, most dogs grow out of this behavior. Administer a time-out and leave the room if you have to, but do not interact with him and thus encourage the behavior.

THE VALUE OF A TOY BIN

Toy bins are wonderful for dogs — even for dogs who are unsure of how to play. Dogs love to hoard, and it's important to teach them what is theirs and what isn't. There are many items in your home that you don't want your dog to chew on: books, magazines, shoes, the remote control, certain stuffed animals, and children's toys. Your dog will not know which toys or items belong to him unless you teach him by providing him with a toy bin.

There are other benefits to having a toy bin. If an object stays on the floor and nobody wants it or uses it, it loses its value for your dog. If a guest comes over and you want to redirect your dog to a toy or encourage him to play, he will have no interest in playing with a toy that has been left untouched on the floor. By keeping his toys in a bin, you will not only increase their value, but you will also be able to direct your dog to his bin to play with his toys when you want to teach him not to jump on your friends or chew on your sofa.

Keep your dog's toys in a large, shallow bin — a plastic storage box works well. Your dog should be able to choose the toys he likes. If the bin is too deep he might not be able to find his favorite toys. When your dog is finished playing with his toys, put them back in the bin. Rotate your dog's toy selection every few weeks or whenever he loses interest in them. After a few weeks, you can act as if old toys are new, and your dog will likely be interested in them again. This makes toys last longer and saves you money. Occasionally put cookies in the bin. If your dog is chewing your sofa or chasing you or wanting to play in a way that you find unacceptable, redirect him to his toys and praise him every time he gets a toy from his bin. You want him to play with his toys, so make a fuss and give him lots of attention when he does!

SUMMARY

Discouraging Jumping, Chewing, and Play-Biting

- Memorize the statement "Life happens on all fours." Give your dog all the attention that he desires and deserves, but only when he has all four paws on the ground.
- The instant your dog jumps on you, remove eye contact and pivot away from him. Do so even when seated.
- Be calm when you open the door to greet guests. Teach your dog to wait at the doorway, or redirect him to an activity away from the door if you don't want him jumping on visitors.

- Your dog will jump less when he carries something in his mouth, such as a ball, toy, or bone.

- Teach your dog that the presence or arrival of strangers and guests results in getting food treats and attention when he sits or lies down.

- While speaking with another person, give your dog treats for standing, sitting, or lying down to reinforce and reward appropriate, calm behavior.

- All puppies and young dogs naturally want to mouth and play-bite. They want to explore their environments with their mouths. Fill a bin with toys and use it to teach your dog what is appropriate for him to chew on. Redirect your dog to his toys when he chews on something that you don't want him to chew on.

- Mist all-natural concentrated orange spray on anything that you do not want your dog to chew. Never use synthetic chemical sprays.

- To eliminate play-biting and to soften your dog's bite, yelp the instant he bites you too hard and give him a brief time-out. Stop making eye contact with him or leave the room.

- If you try to eliminate play-biting too soon, especially in puppies under three months of age, you may fail to teach them how to bite softly.

- If your dog bites at your clothing or legs, stop moving. Be boring. Mist yourself with all-natural orange spray if your puppy persists. Most young dogs grow out of this behavior.

- By keeping your dog's toys in a bin, you will not only increase their value, but you will also be able to direct your dog to his bin when you want to teach him not to jump on your friends or chew on your sofa.

DISCOURAGING BARKING

If your dog seems to bark continually, try to figure out why. Is he afraid? Does he want your attention? Is he happy, lonely, or anxious? The key to solving barking problems is to understand why your dog is barking in the first place.

Attention-Seeking Barking

Attention-seeking barking refers to those times when your dog barks at you to interact with you or to get something from you. The first response should be to increase your dog's exercise. A tired dog is a relaxed dog, and a relaxed dog barks less. A long morning walk or run or an hour of interactive play will release some of your dog's pent-up energy and frustration. It will be easier for you to give him attention when he is quiet and not barking.

Try to anticipate his barks, and redirect his attention or ask him to perform a behavior that is incompatible with barking *before* he starts. Instruct your dog to lie down, or redirect him to another activity. Make these alternate behaviors rewarding for him.

Give your dog food-dispensing toys to keep him busy during the day, especially when you are not home. If he is physically and mentally stimulated, he will be less anxious and bark less. Treat-dispensing toys should be washed out regularly to prevent mold.

Only give your dog attention or make eye contact with him when he is *not* barking, in other words, when he is quiet. Be careful not to reward him for anything too soon after a bark, or you could end up reinforcing the barking.

Try reverse psychology. The instant your dog barks, offer him something that he has no interest in.

Leave the room and give your dog a time-out when he barks. The best way to give a time-out is to cue it. Give your dog one warning as soon as he barks. He will have no idea what your warning means and will continue to bark at you. Then immediately cue his time-out by saying "That's it," "Done," or "I'm outta here," and leave the room. Time-outs should last no more than two minutes.

Barking in the House Out of Boredom

If your dog is barking because he is bored, increase his exercise and play interactive games with him. Your dog should be walked at least two or three times a day. Feed him meals with treat-dispensing toys.

If your dog is barking at something outside, acknowledge the bark by looking out the window to see what he is barking at. Then thank him and direct him away from the window. Repeat this two to three times. If he continues to bark, say "Ah-Ah" and close the blinds or shades immediately when he starts.

Praise and reward your dog for doing something that is incompatible with barking, such as chewing on or playing with a toy, lying down, or being brushed.

Before your dog starts barking or right after he begins, redirect him by giving him all-natural, unsalted peanut butter (avoid processed peanut butters with corn syrup). He will lick the roof of his mouth instead of barking. You can also do this when he barks at you for attention. Just make sure you don't give him peanut butter every time he barks at you, or he might start barking at you just to get the peanut butter.

Barking at Others Out of Fear or While Outside on the Leash

If your dog barks out of fear, pair highly desirable treats with whatever it is that frightens him. Play with him with his favorite toy or do something else with him that he enjoys. Be relaxed. Praise him when he is attentive to you and not barking. Keep him at a comfortable distance from the threat so that he feels relaxed and less anxious. The less anxious he is, the less he will bark. If he is afraid of strangers, ask people to ignore him. They can casually toss him treats but should not stare at him or try to interact with or pet him.

Give your dog treats for paying attention to you and looking at you. Reinforce any and all eye contact he gives you.

Teach your dog to perform other behaviors, such as lying down, looking at you, walking next to you, or sitting when he is in the presence of something that makes him anxious. Reward him generously when he shows you these behaviors.

Practice a removal technique. I call this a "do-over." When your dog barks, say "Ah-Ah" and calmly remove him so he cannot see the trigger. If you have an incessant or emotional barker, you may need to repeat this multiple times. Stay very calm and relaxed as you guide him away. You can walk him in the opposite direction from what he is barking at or into another room. When he is quiet for three to five seconds, praise him. Then walk back toward what triggered him to bark. Praise and reward him generously for not barking. *Keep him at a comfortable and safe distance so that he does not feel threatened or anxious.*

Praise and reward your dog when he does not bark. Reward him for showing calm or happy behavior in the presence of what might make him anxious or afraid.

Do not push your dog into situations that make him uncomfortable. Set him up for success.

SUMMARY

Discouraging Barking

- The key to resolving barking issues is to figure out why your dog is barking.
- A tired dog will be relaxed and bark less.
- Give your dog attention when he is not barking. If he barks at you continually, more than likely you have been reinforcing his barking.
- Try to anticipate a bark and redirect your dog to an activity that is incompatible with barking.
- If your dog is barking because he is scared, pair especially good treats or other rewards with whatever it is that he finds scary. Praise and reward him for performing other behaviors, such as looking at and walking with you.
- Reward your dog when he is quiet. Do not encourage barking by reacting to him when he barks. Don't yell at him — especially if he wants your attention.
- Praise and reward your dog for showing any calm, relaxed, or happy behaviors in the presence of what might make him bark or be reactive.
- If your dog barks at something out the window, acknowledge the bark by looking out the window to see what it is he is barking at. Thank him and direct him away from the window. If he continues to bark, say "Ah-Ah" and close the shades or blinds.
- Practice the "do-over," a removal technique. If your dog barks at something, calmly walk him away from the trigger. When he is quiet, wait three seconds and then praise him. Then walk him back toward the trigger so that he can

see it. Keep him at a comfortable distance so that he does not feel anxious or threatened.

- Do not push your dog into situations that he can't handle or that make him uncomfortable. If he can't handle the situation he will continue to bark. Set him up for success.

HOUSETRAINING

Housetraining a dog — whether a puppy or an older dog — takes patience and consistency. Dogs cannot be housetrained overnight, however much we might want to see this happen. Fortunately, dogs can be housetrained within a few weeks or months — as opposed to human children, who often take a few years to be toilet trained. The principles of toilet training children and housetraining dogs are very similar.

Never punish your dog for peeing or pooping — regardless of the location. Punishment will only scare him, and he will become afraid of urinating or defecating in front of you. If he will not eliminate in front of you, it will be difficult for you to reward him for going in the right location.

Housetraining can be summarized in three steps:

1. Set your dog up for success by establishing a location in which you would like him to eliminate.
2. Make it rewarding for him to pee or poop in that location.
3. Ensure that he never has an opportunity to eliminate in an undesirable location by supervising him and managing his environment.

Here are the steps in more detail.

When you are not able to supervise your dog directly you should confine him to an area small enough that he will not want to urinate or defecate there. Dogs do not want to pee or poop where they eat or sleep or in any other personal spaces or living areas. You can gate off part of a room or use an ex-pen (indoor fencing made for dogs) to restrict an area for your dog to stay in. Make sure this area is comfortable for your dog and has a soft surface or dog bed for him to lie down on. He should be able to stand up, comfortably turn around, lie down, and stretch.

Since dogs prefer not to go to the bathroom in their living areas, your dog must have access to the areas in your home where you would like him to be housetrained. You can tether him to you when you are at home by hooking a leash to your waist. This way he can follow you when you change rooms and will have access to all the rooms of the house where you want him to be. You will be able to see the signs indicating that he has to go to the bathroom, such as pacing, randomly sniffing, whimpering, looking at you, play-biting you, or squatting. If you spend most of your time in one room, gate off that room so that your dog doesn't have access to other areas of the house. Whenever your dog pees or poops in a certain location, he learns from that experience and may come to prefer "pottying" there — especially if you don't remove the odors.

Instead of randomly taking your dog to the place that you have chosen for him to go to the bathroom, take him at times that he is likely to have to go. Most dogs tend to urinate ten to thirty minutes after they drink and to defecate ten to forty minutes after they eat. Young puppies, however, will not be able to hold it that long. All dogs tend to pee or poop immediately on waking (even from a quick nap); after play and exercise; during or immediately following anxious, exciting, or stressful situations such as a car ride or a visit from a friend; and before going to sleep at night.

Teach your dog a word that indicates the location — either

outside or on a pee pad — where you would like him to go to the bathroom. Say the word in an upbeat tone just before or while you are taking him to that location. Note: If you are teaching your dog to urinate and defecate indoors on pee pads (indoor housetraining pads made for dogs), make sure to designate a word for the room or area the pads are in, and for the pad itself. This way your dog will know both where you want him to go and on what surface you would like him to go. Most pee pads, or "wee wee" pads, as they are frequently called, are too small for most dogs to target. Make sure to overlap multiple pads to provide your dog with a larger surface when housetraining him indoors.

Also, teach your dog words for urinating and defecating. Cue words can be "Potty," "Park it," "Hurry up," "Pee-pee," or "Poo-poo." You get the idea! While your dog is peeing or pooping, say the words you have chosen. He will eventually learn to eliminate on hearing your words.

Give your dog an especially good food treat after he pees or poops in the desired location. This treat should be something mouth-watering that he gets only when he urinates or defecates where you want him to. Dogs do not know the value of hardwood floors or Oriental rugs. Without training, your dog has no real motivation to wait to relieve himself. Urinating and defecating feel good to him, and delaying elimination is uncomfortable and unhealthy. By giving your dog an especially good food treat after he eliminates, you are increasing his motivation to go outside or on a pad. Give him a lot of praise when he pees or poops in the proper location.

When taking your dog outside to eliminate, linger in one area. Do not go for a walk or keep changing locations. It will be easier for him to learn to go to the bathroom in a specific area if you keep taking him to the same general place.

Take your dog for a walk *after* he urinates. You can use walking and playing as rewards. If you routinely end a walk or take your dog inside after he pees or poops, he may learn to hold it so that he can keep walking or stay outdoors. Keep in mind that walking stimulates the digestive tract. Often dogs will defecate after they exercise or have walked a little bit.

Let your dog sniff! By sniffing, your dog will want to cover scents or mark, especially if he smells another dog's urine. In addition, sniffing is a great stress reliever for dogs.

Put your dog on a consistent feeding schedule. Do not leave him a bowl of food to nibble at will. If you do not know how much or how often he is eating, you will have trouble predicting when he has to go to the bathroom. Whether you feed him snacks throughout the day or only feed him at mealtimes, you must be aware of when and how much he has eaten. It is not fair to your dog if he is relying on you to take him outside and you do not know when he needs to go.

If your dog eliminates in an inappropriate location, use a cleaner containing enzymes specifically designed to eliminate odors. Products such as Anti-Icky Poo and Simple Solution work well. Do not use household cleaning products such as ammonia, vinegar, carpet deodorizers, Febreze, or Woolite. These may mask odors temporarily but do not break down the odors at their source. In addition, urine contains ammonia. If you use ammonia on soiled areas, you will only encourage your dog to urinate in those locations.

If you catch your dog pottying in an area where you don't want him to eliminate, get his attention *before* he finishes, say your word for the location in which you want him to go, and rush him to the place you have chosen. Then praise him and give him treats for peeing or pooping in the desired location.

Never punish or reprimand your dog for urinating or defecating. He will begin peeing or pooping when you are not looking because he will become afraid to urinate or defecate in front of you.

Your dog will need a way to let you know that he has to potty — especially if he is expected to eliminate outside. Teach him a way to let you know when he needs to go. It is up to you to pay attention to his signals.

Teaching Your Dog to Ring a Bell

Some common behaviors that may indicate that your dog needs to eliminate include walking in circles, wandering, standing or walking by the door, looking at the door, mouthing you, barking at you, or staring at you. If your dog looks perplexed or seems to be trying to find something to do, more than likely he needs to pee or poop.

If your dog isn't housetrained, it is best to assume that any unfocused behavior is a sign that he needs to go potty. Even if you're occasionally wrong, every time that you are right you will successfully encourage your dog to eliminate where you want him to.

Teach your dog to ring a bell. Most dogs can learn to do this fairly easily. This is a nice way for your dog to let people know that he wants to be let outside. Hang a bell on the doorknob of the door that you use to take your dog outside. Sleigh bells work well. The bells will ring every time the door opens, and your dog will learn to associate the sound of the bells with the door. Be sure that he can reach at least one bell; he will need to be able to nudge it with his muzzle.

Show your dog the bell before you take him outside. Ring the bell by tapping it at his nose level with your hand. Say "Outside" (or whatever word you have chosen to designate the area in which you want him to go), and open the door. At some point your dog will ring the bell on his own. The instant he does, celebrate! Say your word and immediately take him outside.

Your dog will not automatically understand that he is supposed to ring the bell if he needs to urinate or defecate. The first time he rings the bell, you will probably be thrilled. Consequently, your dog may ring the bell to get your attention. He may want to go outside to play and not necessarily have to pee or poop. If you have a fenced-in location where he can run freely, this arrangement may work for you. Regardless of why he rings the bell, however, you must take him outside when he rings it. If you take him outside and he does not have to pee or poop, take him back inside and make sure that he doesn't go somewhere you don't want him to. Then try again.

If your dog gets into the habit of ringing the bell just to get your attention, do not automatically assume he does not need to potty when he rings the bell. If you ignore him, it will likely turn out that he really did need to pee or poop, and you will have a big mess to clean up.

SUMMARY

Housetraining

- Housetraining can be summarized in three steps: 1) Manage your dog's environment so that he is unable to potty where you do not want him to. 2) Give your dog many opportunities to eliminate in the location that you have chosen. 3) Make it rewarding for him to pee or poop in that location.

- Teach your dog a word for the location that you have chosen and words for peeing and pooping.
- Give your dog a highly desirable treat immediately after he eliminates in the location you have chosen.
- Do not punish your dog for eliminating in a place you do not want him using.
- Use odor eliminators containing enzymes on areas of the carpet and floor that your dog has soiled.
- Dogs tend to urinate or defecate immediately on waking from naps, after drinking and eating, when stressed or excited, during and following exercise and play, and before going to sleep at night.
- When taking your dog outside to eliminate, keep taking him to the same general location
- Feed your dog on a consistent schedule. Do not leave food out for your dog to nibble at will.
- Teach your dog to ring a bell so that he can signal to you when he needs to be let outside.

STOOL EATING (COPROPHAGIA)

Some dogs and puppies eat their own or another dog's stools. There are different theories as to why dogs do this, but to my knowledge, there are no definite conclusions. This behavior can be a problem with small dogs who are housetrained on pee pads. Some dogs simply outgrow it. Many taste-aversive products don't seem very effective, and so you might want to try several of the following strategies.

Dogs who eat stools may be lacking something in their diets, often raw food that contains cellulose and fiber. Many packaged dog foods do not contain enough of the life-giving energy that animals need. Often dogs who eat poop also eat a lot of grass, shove sticks or rocks in their mouths, and eat dirt, sometimes frantically. If your dog is exhibiting any of these behaviors, make his diet more holistic and nutritious by adding cellulose and fiber. Any kind of plant food, such as brown rice, dark green lettuce, carrots, a spoonful of canned pumpkin, spinach, and other vegetables, will do. You can also add papain or vegetarian digestive enzymes to your dog's food.

Dogs who eat their food too quickly may eat their own poop. When a dog eats too fast, much of the food can remain undigested, and whole pieces of food can be found in his feces. Encourage your dog to eat more slowly by feeding him handfuls of kibble in succession or multiple small portions at mealtimes. You can also put his food in treat-dispensing toys or in bowls that make eating more challenging for him. These toys and bowls can be found in pet supply stores.

Sometimes stool-eating is a learned behavior. This means your dog learns it by watching another dog. When a behavior is learned, it can become a habit. The less frequently your dog exhibits this behavior, the less likely it is that it will continue. Teach your dog alternate behaviors to perform after he or another dog defecates. You can teach him to come to you and sit for a food treat after he or another dog poops, or you can teach him to "Leave it" by using an interruption such as "Ah-Ah" or "Hey" and then rewarding him for backing away from the poop.

By all means, try taste-aversive products. As far as I know, they are safe. Just don't be too disheartened if they don't seem to work. If they do, celebrate. Adding a teaspoon of pineapple to your dog's food may help. Forbid and meat tenderizer are popular taste aversives. Also, try to pick up stools before your dog has a chance to eat them.

Chapter Five

BEHAVIOR MODIFICATION FOR DOGS WHO EXHIBIT FEAR, AGGRESSION, AND ANXIETY

PREVENT AND MANAGE

Fearful and aggressive dogs need help. You should never reprimand or scold your dog when he is frightened or nervous. Growling, snarling, crying, panting, and whining are emotional reactions. These behaviors may annoy you, but reprimanding your dog for exhibiting them will not address the source of the problem. Always try to be as gentle and positive with your dog as you can. He can conquer his fears — but only with your help.

An aggressive dog requires more management. You must prevent the events that trigger your dog's aggression, and you need to protect him and other people, dogs, and animals from injury. Aggression stems from fear and anxiety. Once you find out why your dog is stressed and anxious, you will be better able to rectify his aggression. Work with a humane trainer or behaviorist on any aggression issue that makes you uncomfortable.

When you are not able to actively work on alleviating your dog's fears or anxieties, try not to expose him to whatever it is that makes him nervous. If you expose him to things that frighten him or make him anxious you will simply reinforce fearful or anxious behavior. If he becomes fearful in specific situations and you let these situations continue to occur, you will not be doing anything to improve his physical, mental, or emotional state.

HOW TO HELP A FEARFUL OR AGGRESSIVE DOG

Desensitize your dog to whatever causes him stress. Expose him gradually to things that make him nervous, but do so at a pace or level that doesn't cause him to get upset or to become reactive. If your dog seems upset or anxious in any way when exposed to triggers that previously caused him stress, you are not desensitizing him.

Countercondition your dog to what makes him nervous by changing his associations with his stressors to make them positive and pleasurable for him. You can do this by pairing things that he dislikes with things that he loves. When you expose your dog to a low-level stressor (desensitization), pair it with something he adores, such as food, baby talk, walks, play, toys, or gentle touch. The positive experience that you provide for him should be more potent than the stressor he is being exposed to. The goal is to lead him to enjoy what he initially disliked. This is not bribery. You are changing your dog's perception of what used to make him nervous.

You will need to provide your dog with highly desirable food or treats when working through his fears. Use whole food instead of processed dog snacks. Some dogs like carob and molasses treats. Dogs also tend to prefer soft foods over crunchy ones. Every dog has certain preferences. If your dog has a medical condition or requires a special diet, please meet with a holistic veterinarian to see if there is something you can give him that will allow you to implement behavior modification techniques at home.

Do not get angry or tense if your dog growls. Be positive and calm. Redirect him from the negative experience to a behavior that is rewarding for you both. Avoid stressful situations that cause him to growl or become upset by managing his environment so that these situations do not repeatedly occur.

Watch your body language. Never approach or confront a fearful dog. A dog who is afraid of a person or another dog should always be the one to approach or initiate interactions. A fearful dog should never be directly confronted with what frightens him.

Always position yourself at an angle to fearful dogs. Stand or kneel parallel or at a perpendicular angle to them. Facing dogs and staring at them can make them frightened or anxious. As mentioned earlier, petting your dog directly on the head can be threatening and may make him uncomfortable. Pet him under his chin or on his chest and angle your body away from him as you approach or pet him, especially if he is fearful.

FIGURE 36. Angling away from Kiva as I kneel down and look at her encourages her to look at me and approach. This body position is great for dogs who are fearful or dogs who are reluctant to approach on leash.

FIGURE 37. Angling my body slightly away from Bessie and Jake causes them to look at me and orient in my direction.

Direct eye contact unnerves dogs. Never stare down a dog. It will not establish your dominance, and you will only scare or intimidate him. Your dog will appreciate it if you look away at times or look at him without staring.

Never jerk your dog with the leash. Leash jerks can cause tension and fear and will just make your dog more reactive. The more you jerk your dog on leash, the less he will look at you. If you get stressed when you are out with your dog, walk or run with an iPod and listen to your favorite music. You will remain calmer and not put off as much nervous energy. This may help your dog relax, and he will find it easier to pay attention to you.

If your dog is fearful or nervous around strangers, pair people with positive experiences for him. People can give your dog treats when he approaches them or can toss them to him. If he is overly nervous or anxious around strangers, ask them to ignore him. You may need to be the one to give him treats if accepting food directly from strangers is too scary for him.

If your dog gets nervous when you have company over, designate a place where he can go to feel safe. This place should have a positive association for him, and no one should intrude on him while he is there.

Products such as Comfort Zone (dog-appeasing pheromone), melatonin, and/or pharmaceutical medication may help alleviate your dog's anxiety. Speak with your veterinarian if you are interested in pharmacological intervention.

Help for Dogs Who Are Fearful or Reactive on Leash

Knowing how to get and maintain your dog's attention and eye contact, teaching him good recall skills, and learning how to hold the leash properly (so it stays relaxed around his neck) will all help if your dog is fearful or aggressive.

Front-clip harnesses such as the Sense-ation are good to have when working with fearful or aggressive dogs. Head halters, such as the Gentle Leader, can be useful when managing aggressive dogs who may have a tendency to bite people or other animals. A martingale-style collar can help if you have a fearful dog who pulls out of his collar. Attention exercises can help countercondition your dog to eye contact if eye contact makes him nervous or uncomfortable (see page 32).

If your dog is reactive or fearful when on the leash, you can position him in ways that are more comfortable for him when outside in stressful situations. The four positions described on pages 108–10 can help lessen your dog's fearful or aggressive responses. They will make him feel safer and more secure. Note: Even when you have to shorten the leash (see pages 123–24), try to keep it relaxed when you guide him away from or past what stresses or frightens him. Encourage him to look at you and follow you through the use of food lures, praise and other rewards, such as running and playing tug.

• Position yourself between your dog and the stressor. This makes your dog feel more secure. Feed him treats as he passes by what stresses or frightens him.

FIGURE 38. Positioning yourself between your dog and a distraction will keep him more engaged and focused on you.

FIGURE 39. Positioning yourself between your dog and what stresses him will make him feel more comfortable and attentive.

- Position your dog so that his back is to the stressor and he is facing you. When a dog turns his back to another dog or a person, he is signaling that he does not want to interact or engage in a confrontation. This is a good way to diffuse a situation if the stressor is close by. In addition, by facing in your direction, he will be more attentive to you and look to you for guidance. Give him lots of treats and praise him while he waits for what frightens him to pass.

FIGURE 40. Positioning your dog's back to a stressor will keep him calmer and more relaxed.

FIGURE 41. Positioning Sebby's back to Andy and Marilyn while I treat him keeps his focus on me, and he is less distracted.

- Make a U-turn and walk in the opposite direction of the stressor. Don't force your dog to experience something he can't handle. Before you turn, get your dog's attention in a positive way, and then reward him for turning with you.
- Walk in a large semicircle around the stressor, increasing the distance between your dog and the stressor.

Do not use choke, pinch, or shock collars when working with a fearful or aggressive dog. Harsh training techniques or reactive and aggressive behavior from you will intensify your dog's fearfulness or aggression.

STAGES OF WORKING WITH REACTIVE AND FEARFUL DOGS

There are several stages to working with fearful and aggressive dogs and applying desensitization and counterconditioning techniques, and these stages may overlap. The first stage consists of pairing experiences your dog loves with whatever scares or frightens him. If he is too fearful or reactive or will not accept the treats or goodies that you provide, he is overwhelmed. Either you are exposing him to more than he can handle, or the treats you are offering are not especially desirable. If you are applying desensitization and counterconditioning techniques correctly, your dog will come to associate the food or rewards that you provide with the experience that previously stressed him and will begin to look forward to that experience.

Once your dog anticipates getting treats or being rewarded during a stressful situation, he will make eye contact with you and may appear calmer or happier around the stressor.

Then you can proceed to the second stage. Begin giving your dog copious treats for performing nonreactive behaviors, such as paying attention to you; being relaxed, calm, or happy; or sitting or lying down. He should not be as fearful or anxious as he used to be.

FIGURE 42. Rewarding Sebby while passing other dogs makes passing them enjoyable to him.

Once he seems calmer or happier, you can move to the third stage and reinforce behaviors such as sitting, being in a relaxed down position, staying and settling, coming, and so on. At this stage, you can teach him what you would like him to do when a stressor is present. Your dog should be able to look to you for guidance and feel comfortable around his previous stressor. He may want to do something to earn rewards. Do you want him to look at you when other dogs pass? Would you like him to sit at the curb while cars pass or give you a high five and make eye contact? Do you want him to lie down next to you when a guest comes over or to go to his safe area in another room?

During the final stage of this process, if your dog was fearful of other dogs or people, you might begin to expose him to a group setting, such as taking him on a doggy picnic or hike with family or friends, or attending a positive dog training class together.

SUMMARY

Behavior Modification for Dogs Who Are Fearful and Aggressive

- If you are not able to work on alleviating your dog's fears, don't expose him to what makes him nervous.
- Fearful and aggressive dogs need help. Dogs should never be reprimanded or scolded for being frightened.
- Aggressive dogs require more management. Protect your dog from exposure to his stressor, and keep him, other dogs or animals, and other people from getting hurt.
- Do not get angry or tense if your dog growls, but be positive and calm, and direct him away from the negative experience.
- Desensitize and countercondition your dog to those things that make him anxious or upset.
- You will need to give your dog highly desirable treats and rewards as you work through his fears.
- Watch your body language around fearful dogs. Always position yourself at an angle to a fearful dog. Encourage friends and family to do the same.
- Direct eye contact and staring unnerves dogs. *Never* stare down dogs. It will only make them feel insecure, fearful, or aggressive.
- Reward your dog for making eye contact by doing the attention exercises (see page 32). This can be helpful if he is afraid to make eye contact with you or becomes fearful when people look at him.

- A head halter can help you manage your dog so that he cannot bite someone. A front-clip harness can help prevent him from lunging or pulling on the leash.
- Never jerk on the leash or use pinch, shock, or choke collars.
- If your dog is scared of strangers, designate a place where he can go to feel safe when you have company over.
- Learn proper leash techniques so that you can position your dog in a way that is more comfortable for him when he is exposed to a stressful situation.
- Get the support of a humane, qualified behaviorist or trainer for help resolving your dog's fear or aggression issues.

SEPARATION ANXIETY

You can apply the principles of desensitization and counterconditioning to prevent your dog from becoming anxious when someone he is attached to leaves or when he is left alone. Pair your absence with something positive that will keep your dog busy for most, if not all, of the time that you are gone. When you reappear, remove the treats you gave him when you left. You want your dog to want you to leave the house.

Your dog should not be left alone unless you are able to pair a positive experience with your absence. You may have to hire a pet sitter, ask a friend to watch your dog, or take your dog to a doggy-daycare facility or playgroup while you are away. If your dog is the only animal in the household, adding a second dog to the family may help.

Expose your dog to the experience of being left alone for only short periods of time; start with a few seconds. If he becomes nervous, anxious, or fearful before you leave, pair positive experiences with cues for your departure, such as having a cup of coffee or putting on a sweater. The instant you cue your departure, give your dog a highly desirable treat. He should be occupied by the treat most, if not all, of the time it takes you to have a cup of coffee or put on your sweater.

Some other techniques that may help remedy separation anxiety include teaching your dog how to play interactive games, such as "go find" games and scavenger hunts. These games can keep him entertained while you are gone. Give him toys that dispense treats when you leave the house.

Do not ignore your dog when you return, but do not be too excited either. Also, if you are upset when you leave, your dog will be even more upset than usual when he's alone.

Increase your dog's exercise. If you exercise your dog before you leave, he will be more relaxed and may even take a nap when you are gone. Taking morning hikes, running, biking, and playing with other dogs are all good forms of exercise.

Leave your dog in a comfortable location. Do not put him in a crate to resolve separation anxiety. Putting him in a crate to prevent damage to your property will not resolve his fear or anxiety issues and can, in fact, make his anxiety worse. If you do come home and find things damaged, do not reprimand or punish your dog. This will only contribute to his anxiety.

Spend time positively teaching your dog. Humane training gives dogs confidence, enhances their ability to communicate with you, and keeps them stimulated.

Country, classical music, and nature CDs may also help dogs relax.

If your dog's separation anxiety is severe, medication may be helpful. Please speak with your veterinarian.

Professional help is valuable when resolving any behavioral

problem. Please see a professional animal behaviorist if you have a dog with severe separation anxiety.

FEAR OF THUNDERSTORMS AND FIREWORKS

Another source of anxiety for dogs is loud, unexpected sounds such as thunder and fireworks. Here are several tips to ease your dog's anxiety before or during a storm or when fireworks are scheduled:

- Use reverse psychology. Try to make thunderstorms and fireworks positive for your dog. Don't act as if something is wrong or continually try to soothe him; this will just validate his fears. Try to pair thunderstorms and fireworks with things that your dog really loves. Be gentle and positive. Stay relaxed.
- If your dog will eat, give him treats continually during fireworks or storms. Pick food that really makes his mouth water. He may be too nervous to eat at first, but if the food is highly desirable he might try it.
- Teach your dog to go to a safe location where you know he feels comfortable. Choose a place away from windows or the outer walls of the house so that sounds are muffled and he does not have to hear windows rattle.
- Install a Comfort Zone pheromone diffuser in the area your dog will be in during storms or fireworks.
- Muffle noise by turning on the television or playing the radio, and closing blinds, curtains, and windows. If your dog will tolerate it, place cotton balls in his ears. Be careful not to put the cotton balls too far into his ear canals, and don't forget to remove them when the storm is over.

- Feed your dog a carbohydrate-rich meal before a storm. Potatoes, brown rice, or pasta may help him relax and make him feel sleepy.
- Massage your dog during a storm or fireworks. Gentle soothing touch can calm dogs and help them to relax.
- To comfort your dog, appear calm and relaxed. Try not to be overly consoling; this will simply reinforce his anxiety.
- Special capes designed for dogs who are frightened during storms are available from www.stormdefender.com. These capes, which protect dogs from static electricity, help some dogs remain calm. Dogs may also find the weight of the capes soothing. Anxiety wraps, which are sold at www.anxietywrap.com, may also help dogs relax.

CAR SICKNESS

Many dogs get carsick. After one or two bad experiences, your dog may get anxious or nauseous just looking at a car. You can try spraying Comfort Zone in the car to relax him.

Expose your dog to the car gradually, and pair the exposure with something positive. Stop exposing him to the car before he becomes stressed or upset. This may mean giving him treats as you approach the car. When you turn around and walk away from the car, stop giving him treats. You can also try giving him treats as he gets into the car or as you start the engine. When you turn off the engine, or when your dog gets out of the car, stop giving him treats.

You may want to begin by simply spending time with your dog in the car. Give him treats and play with him while keeping the engine off. Then go for a brief walk. This may be a day's training. Expose your dog to the car gradually, until he feels comfortable taking short car rides. Initially these car rides might be only two to five minutes long.

When taking a car ride with your dog, keep the windows partially open to allow fresh air to circulate, or keep the air conditioner running. Defrost or heat from the car can intensify your dog's queasy feeling.

Take your dog for short car rides to fun places. If your dog goes to the vet or the groomer every time he's in the car, he will learn to associate car rides with unpleasant experiences.

Sometimes being in a crate can intensify car sickness for dogs. Use a dog seatbelt or car harness instead of a crate, and keep your dog toward the front of the car to prevent nausea.

Cocculus is a good homeopathic remedy for car sickness and can be found in many natural food stores. Pepcid, or famotidine, can be bought over the counter and may also help. Dramamine will not cure car sickness and may cause drowsiness.

Pull over if your dog gets ill. Take him for a brief walk and give him some fresh air.

Take your dog for walks before and after riding in the car. Do not feed him before going on car rides.

Chapter Six

WALKING ON A RELAXED LEASH, THE SIT-DOWN STRIKE, AND TEACHING YOUR DOG TO WAIT

TOOLS TO HELP WITH WALKING YOUR DOG

The right tools can make it easier to walk a dog who pulls, without using aversive methods.

A Sof-touch leash has a bit of elastic at the end, and dogs feel tension in the elastic when they get to the end of the leash. This piece of elastic can prevent a sudden jerk on your dog's neck if you abruptly change direction. Sof-touch leashes are available online at www.webtrail.com/petbehavior. Elastic or bungee leash attachments, such as the Jerk-Ease, can also prevent jerking and make walking more pleasurable.

Front-clip harnesses, such as the Sense-ation Harness (available at www.softouchconcepts.com), Easy-Walk Harness by Premier Pet Products (available in most pet supply stores), and Walk Your Dog with Love Harness, all work on the same principle. The leash attaches to the front of the harness, which will lead your dog to rotate back in your direction if he pulls too far forward. These are humane tools, and most dogs take to them easily. The harnesses are easy to put on and take off. They also can help you to get your dog's attention. Sometimes they can cause chafing — especially with dogs who have little to no hair under their forelegs or who are unaccustomed to wearing harnesses. If the Sense-ation or Easy Walk harness chafes your dog, you can attach a piece of soft fabric, bought at any fabric or craft store, to that strap to soften it. This eliminates the problem. Other body harness styles, such as the Freedom No-Pull Harness by Wiggles, Wags, and Whiskers, the Walkezee, and the Mekuti Balance Harness, are also worth trying. A head halter such as the Canny Collar (available online), Comfort Trainer (also available online), or Halti or Gentle Leader (available in most pet supply stores) can help ease pulling for dogs who for some reason can't wear a harness, or for dogs who may be aggressive or reactive. If you would like to walk two dogs on the same leash, a "coupler" can be used. Make sure dogs never act aggressively toward each other on walks. If they do, a coupler is not recommended.

A head halter, such as the Gentle Leader, can be helpful in managing an aggressive dog. When your dog wears a head halter, you have more control over his muzzle and can prevent him from biting another person or another dog or animal. Make sure to accustom your dog to wearing a head halter by desensitizing him to it before you use one. This can take a few weeks. Make the head halter pleasurable for him by playing his favorite games or giving him yummy treats when he wears it. In addition, make sure to learn proper leash techniques when using a head halter. Always keep the leash relaxed where it connects to the leader, and *never* jerk on a head halter.

Ultimately, rewarding your dog for not pulling on the leash and for walking with you — in other words, rewarding him for checking in by looking at you (see page 33) and walking near or close to you — are the best ways to teach him to stop pulling. Learning how to hold and work with a leash properly so that you do not jerk on his neck is crucial.

HOW TO HOLD AND SHORTEN A LEASH PROPERLY

How you hold the leash is very important when working with a dog who pulls or who is fearful, timid, or aggressive. Improving and developing your leash skills and holding the leash correctly helps you control your dog, prevents you from jerking and yanking on his neck, and frees one of your hands so that you can give him treats or carry something he values on the walk. These basic leash techniques will give you more control over your dog's movements and give him more freedom at the same time.

FIGURE 43. Leash skills.

The Basics

Let the loop or handle of the leash drape over your thumb. This will not only free up the fingers on that hand, but it will also — with proper body alignment and mechanics — leave you with more strength if your dog lunges and pulls. Close your fingers around the leash by making a relaxed fist. When you hold the leash in this way you break the impact of the pull if your dog suddenly lunges or pulls too hard.

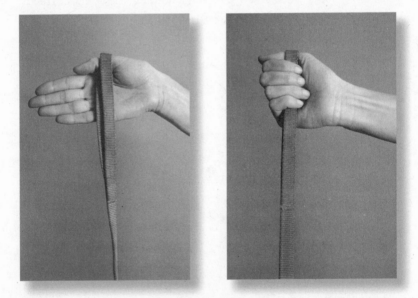

FIGURES 44 and 45. How to hold a leash properly.

It is useless to use only your upper body strength to pull your dog when he lunges with all his weight. If you do, you will have little choice but to yank back on your dog, which will not only reinforce his behavior by making him more reactive and pull against you but may also result in muscle strain in your back and shoulders. If you freeze and tense your muscles, keeping your arms pinned close to your body, your dog will have to pull against your body weight. In addition, by not yanking back on your dog, you will not encourage him to pull you.

Always keep your arm or forearm in line with your dog and at the same angle as the leash. This will prevent injury if your dog suddenly pulls you because he will be pulling against your body weight as opposed to your wrist or forearm.

Because both your hands are free when you hold the leash by looping the handle on your thumb, you can shorten the leash and stay in control of your dog while holding treats, a tennis ball, your car keys, or a clicker.

To shorten the leash, decide how much of it you would like to shorten, and hold that section with the hand that isn't holding the leash. Bring your hand that is holding the leash to meet it, and loop that section over the thumb that is holding the leash handle. It will look as if two leashes are in line on top of each other over your thumb. Secure the leash by closing your fist. This will prevent the leash from slipping out of your hand.

FIGURE 46.
Always keep some fingers on the leash handle as you hold or grab something, such as keys or the poop bag.

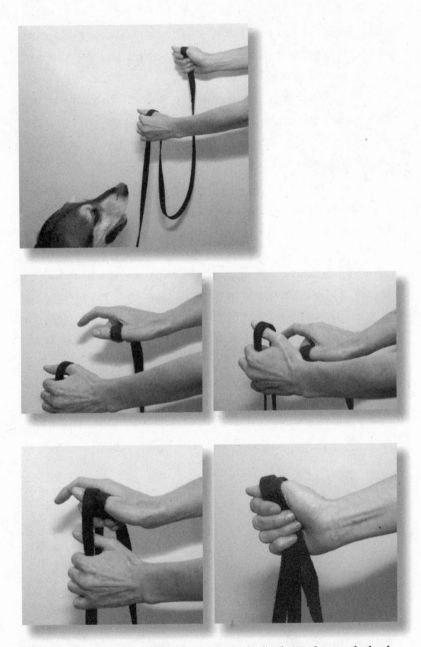

FIGURES 47, 48, 49, 50, 51. Steps to shorten the leash. To shorten the leash more, just repeat the steps.

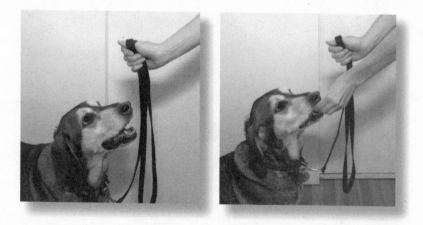

FIGURES 52 and 53. Treating Lucy with my free hand after I shorten the leash. The leash is relaxed at her neck.

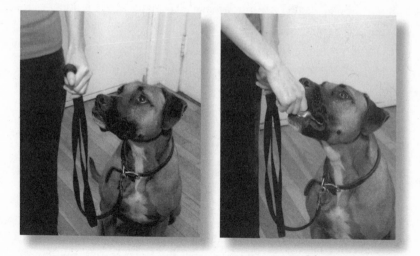

FIGURES 54 and 55. Holding the leash in my left hand as I treat Sebby with my right. Notice the U-shape of the relaxed leash.

FIGURE 56. I've taken two loops to shorten the leash. The leash is relaxed. A relaxed leash will make your dog more attentive to you.

You can shorten the leash without pulling your dog. If he pulls, stop. Walk toward him while you shorten the leash; you can also shorten it as he approaches you. Even though you may walk toward your dog, you do not have to let him continue to pull you. You can give your dog very little leash and still keep it relaxed at his neck. A relaxed leash means that there is no tension on it. The leash clip will sag a little bit or make a U-shape where it attaches to your dog's collar or harness.

You probably tend to lean forward or try to reel your dog in, with both hands on the leash, when he lunges or pulls against you. This puts you off balance and leaves you without a free hand to use to give your dogs treats for performing behaviors you like.

There are two ways you can stand to maintain your balance when your dog suddenly pulls or lunges. You can position yourself with one leg in front of the other and lean your weight on your back leg. Sit back as if you are going to sit down on a chair. You will have more strength because you will be using your legs and lower body — not your upper body or forearms.

The other way is to turn toward the leash so that the length of the leash is in front of you and the side of your body faces your dog. By positioning yourself so that your side faces your dog, you will have more strength and be able to keep him from pulling you or pursuing whatever he is lunging at, without your jerking his leash or pulling him.

FIGURE 57. Resting my weight on my back leg prevents me from leaning forward or jerking on Kiva as she tries to pull me. My arm is in the same direction as Kiva and is in line with the leash.

FIGURE 58. Standing sideways to Kiva with my forearm in front of me enables me to maintain my balance without pulling back on her. My arm is facing Kiva's direction and in line with the leash.

WALKING WITH A RELAXED LEASH

The techniques in this section will help you teach your dog to walk nicely with you while you keep the leash relaxed. They take some practice, but once you feel comfortable with the techniques your dog will pay better attention to you, and you will both have more fun walking together.

As previously mentioned, dogs have an oppositional reflex. If you push or pull one way on your dog, he will instinctively push or pull in the opposite direction. The moment he feels tension on the leash he will naturally want to override it. He will pull against the tension, and in doing so he will pull against you. The more tension he feels and the more you pull back on him, the more he will pull. If you continually pull against him, and he succeeds in going in his direction, he will learn that when he feels resistance on the leash he just has to pull harder to go where he wants to.

FIGURE 59. A great way to feed a dog while walking. Use your open palm!

It is important to teach your dog from the beginning that pulling on you does not make you move forward faster. This means that you can't pull back on him. If you create tension by pulling back on his leash or collar, he will just want to override the tension he feels, and you will reinforce his pulling.

Practice these four principles to teach your dog not to pull you. You will have better control of your dog, without resorting to jerking or yanking on his collar or harness. This will make him more attentive to you.

1. *Reward your dog for looking at you:* Praise your dog, give him treats, and smile at him whenever he glances in your direction or looks at you. When you are outside with your dog, you may notice that he glances at you from time to time. He is checking in with you to take cues from you. Reinforce any eye contact your dog gives you. You do not have to prompt him to look at you. Simply treat and praise him every time he looks at you, and he will look at you more often. To perfect this, treat your dog when he looks at you after any mild distraction, including sniffing the ground or watching a person or dog in the distance, during any distraction that may lose his focus, and when he walks away from you farther than four or five feet on the leash. Praise him when he looks at you. Now you are walking together!

2. *Practice Red Light/Green Light:* Whenever you feel any tension on the leash, instantly stop moving, or tense the muscles in your arm. The quicker you are at this, the better it will work. You should stop for no longer than one or two seconds. Do not pull back on your dog's collar or leash. The instant the leash relaxes and the tension releases,

start walking again. You or your dog can release tension on the leash. If he stops when you stop, take a step closer to him so that the leash relaxes, and then start walking again. Don't expect him to back up. Likewise, if he slows down, stops, or turns his head even slightly and the tension on the leash releases, start walking again. Be quick; if you wait too long you will confuse him. He will eventually check in with you when he gets to the end of the leash by glancing at you or in your direction. This is the first step in teaching him not to pull you. He learns that when he gets to the end of the leash and pulls you, he doesn't go anywhere. He will soon wait, slow down, look at you, or stop when he gets to the end of the leash. Praise him when he does!

FIGURE 60. Red Light: waiting for Lucy to check in.

FIGURE 61. Green Light: praising and then rewarding Lucy for looking at me and walking with me.

3. *Walk in the opposite direction:* Walking away from your dog or in the opposite direction makes you more interesting and will make him pay more attention to you. You can turn this into a game. When he gets to you, reward him and keep moving by changing directions. You can give him treats for looking at you, stopping with you, turning with you, following you, or coming to you. Continue to move in different directions, and encourage him to follow you. Whenever he catches up to you or walks in the same direction as you, reward him.

You cannot teach your dog to follow you on a leash if he is always ahead of you. You also don't want to trick him and jerk him so that he is afraid to move in a different direction than you. You want to teach your dog to follow you voluntarily. If he continues to head in a direction other than the one you chose and ignores your prompts to follow you, he will soon get to the end of the leash and you can implement Red Light/Green Light. If he pulls on the leash, stop moving. Don't pull him. Then encourage him to come to you, follow you, or run with you. Reward him when he does.

4. *Reward your dog for following your lead and guidance:* Behaviors to reinforce in your dog include looking in your direction, not pulling on the leash, walking with you, turning with you, stopping when you do, and looking at you. All these behaviors should be acknowledged, fussed over, and rewarded. If your dog stays by your side as you run or walk, praise him and give him treats. If he turns when you turn, reward him. Let him know when you are going to turn by getting his attention or saying "This way" in a perky voice, so that he can follow you and get rewarded.

Once your dog realizes that the goal is to walk with you on the leash without pulling, allow him to choose the direction you take on your walks. Let him choose where he wants to go and what he wants to see. If he starts to pull you, stop and change direction until he is focused and paying attention to you. Then go back in his original choice of direction. Let him go where he wants to go when the leash is relaxed.

In addition to the four techniques above, you can teach your dog a "Let's go" cue that means you want to start moving again after you both have stopped for a moment. Stand next to your dog. Make a clicking sound or another noise to get him to look at you. Say, "Let's go," and step forward or backward, beginning with the leg closest to him. Treat him when he looks at you, follows you, or turns with you.

FIGURES 62, 63, 64, 65.
Relaxed leash walking.
Turn it into a game.

Finally, let your dog sniff. People often become impatient and jerk on the leash to prevent their dogs from exploring interesting smells, which dogs love to do. If you try to prevent your dog from sniffing too much or you become impatient and drag him, he will more than likely become obsessed with trying to catch any scent that he can. Let him sniff for a few moments. Then say, "Let's go," and reward him for walking with you again. This will make him listen to you more often and be more receptive to your requests. As mentioned earlier, sniffing is a great stress reliever. If your dog is less stressed, he will be better behaved and more relaxed.

Unfortunately, we often teach dogs to pull us, and then we reinforce it. You can undo this habit, but it takes patience and consistency. Remember to practice good leash techniques, and don't jerk on that leash!

DOGS WHO RESIST GOING FOR WALKS, OR THE "SIT-DOWN STRIKE"

I call dogs who resist going on walks "bottom ploppers" and refer to the behavior as a "Sit-Down Strike." If you have a dog who does not want to walk with you, try to figure out why. Is your dog afraid? Is he wary of noises, sirens, cars passing, other dogs, strangers, or kids on bicycles? Did he have a bad experience on a walk? Or does he merely prefer being comfy indoors to the cold, rainy outing you propose? A dog will hesitate to go for walks if he finds walks unpleasant. If your dog has been startled or frightened on a walk, he will be reluctant to risk repeating the experience. If walks continue to be stressful, he may even resist going out for a walk altogether. If your dog runs away from you or hides when he sees you with his leash, he is either fearful of you, the leash, the collar, or some aspect of the walk.

Your dog may appear to be afraid of the leash when he is actually afraid of your direct approach when putting the leash on him.

He may be afraid of face-front body language and being leaned over or grabbed. This is a common problem for little dogs. To resolve it, feed your dog good treats as soon as you get out the leash. Stand next to your dog as you put on his leash and attach the leash to his collar or harness by reaching under his head. Do not lean or hover over your dog or gaze directly at him; instead angle your body away from him as you attach the leash. Your dog will find your body language less threatening, so it will be easier for him to relax. Reward him profusely for letting you put on his leash and then take him outside for the walk.

FIGURE 66. Kneel next to your dog and adjust his collar or harness from under his head, as opposed to standing or leaning over him.

Walks should be fun for your dog, not stressful or burdensome. If you drag your dog when out on walks, prevent him from sniffing, jerk his neck repeatedly with many corrections, or insist that he walk right behind you or flush next to you by keeping him on a tight leash, your dog will dislike walking with you, or may even fear you. Collars such as choke chains and pinch collars can make many dogs reluctant to go on walks or have the collars put on them. These collars are confusing to dogs, and they hurt. If you are dragging your dog out the door and he is wearing one of these collars, the anxiety and pain he experiences will make him dislike walking with you even more. If you lighten up on the leash and use a fabric collar or a comfortable harness instead, he will come to enjoy and look forward to his walks.

Walking too quickly or for too long can make a dog stop and then refuse to budge. Older dogs, dogs who were previously injured, and dogs with back, hip, or knee pain may have a tough time keeping up with you on walks. Likewise, young puppies have little endurance. They tire easily, are not well coordinated, and need frequent breaks. Tired puppies will frequently resist walks and plop their bottoms down, refusing to continue. Encourage your puppy to play and hang out with you in a park or the yard. Pay attention to what your dog is trying to tell you and adjust your expectations for next time. Walk slower if you have a young puppy or older dog. Take him for brief walks around the block and let him go at his own pace.

If your dog sits or stops as you walk ahead of him, kneel down with your back to your dog. Keep the leash relaxed. Do not tug on the leash or pull him along. It will only make the behavior worse because dogs have an oppositional reflex: they will automatically respond to your pulling by pulling back. Instead, look over your shoulder at him a few times, and wait. Don't say anything and be patient. He will come to you. When he comes, praise him and give him a treat. Do this the next two or three times that he stops. When he stops the third or fourth time, do not treat him when he comes to you, just praise him, begin walking, and treat him for walking with you. When you treat him for walking with you, he will walk with you more and stop less. You can also throw cookies ahead of you as you walk, in a variation of the recall game. This game will reward your dog for running ahead of you, instead of for lagging behind. Once you and your dog enjoy walking together, reward him intermittently and less often, but until you and he have perfected the art of walking together, be generous and consistent with rewards. Be sure to vary rewards by playing with him, running with him, or giving him sticks if he likes to carry something. Variety will make your walks fun and interesting.

When you are walking your dog, let him sniff! I frequently see people dragging their dogs, often unintentionally, when their dogs stop to look at something or sniff. Their dogs then plop their bottoms down and stop. This is a common situation with puppies. Be mindful of what your dog is doing. If he wants to potty or smell something interesting, let him. After he is busy for a few minutes doing what he wants to do, jolly him up and encourage him to move along. Reward him when he turns to you and follows you. He will appreciate the overture and will be more responsive to you on future walks.

Dogs are context learners, and they tend to repeat their behaviors in the settings and locations in which they have performed them before. Some dogs may do a Sit-Down Strike when you choose a different route from the one they are familiar with. Dogs like routine; however, if they become too accustomed to a routine, they may become anxious when you try to vary it. Likewise, if your dog decides one day to plop down and stop in a particular location, the next time you revisit that area he may well experience déjà vu and perform his Sit-Down Strike all over again.

If you suspect that your dog has become habituated to Sit-Down Strike in certain locations, avoid these locations for a while, or vary your route to pass in the opposite direction. Encourage your dog to keep moving *before* he experiences his déjà vu moment and repeats his Sit-Down Strike. You can do this by treating,

feeding, and verbally motivating him, or by engaging him in a distracting and fun activity, such as running, toy squeaking, or stick
tossing. If you wait to entice him after he decides to stop walking,
you might get stuck trying to coerce him with bribery, which seldom works and is never a long-term solution! If you have a little
dog, you can easily pick him up and carry him for a few steps or
a few blocks if he keeps on resisting. But for those who have large
dogs, this isn't an option.

If your dog seems to be afraid of the outdoors or anxious
about events that may occur on walks, read chapter 5 on how to
desensitize and countercondition your dog to these triggers.

SUMMARY

Walking on a Relaxed Leash and the Sit-Down Strike

- A Sof-touch leash has an elastic band near the end that
  helps prevent a sudden jerk on your dog's neck if you stop
  abruptly or suddenly change direction. You can also pur-
  chase elastic leash attachments, such as Jerk-Ease.
- A front-clip harness such as a Sense-ation, Easy Walk,
  Walk Your Dog with Love Harness, or Wonder Walker,
  can make it easier walking a dog who pulls. Other harnesses, such as the Freedom Harness, Mekuti Balance
  Harness, and Walkezee, can also work well.
- Head halters, such as a Canny Collar, Halti, Gentle Leader,
  or Comfort Halter may help for dogs who for some
  reason cannot wear a harness. A head halter, such as
  the Gentle Leader, can be helpful when managing aggressive dogs.

- Rewarding your dog for not pulling on the leash and for walking with you are the best ways to teach him to stop pulling. Reward your dog for looking at you, walking next to you, stopping when you do, and turning with you.

- A relaxed leash means that there is no tension on the leash where it attaches to your dog's collar or harness. You can keep him on a very short leash and still keep it relaxed around his neck.

- Practicing Red Light/Green Light, walking in a different direction from your dog, and rewarding him for paying attention to you, following you, and turning with you are good ways to teach him to stop pulling.

- If your dog lunges on the leash, tense your muscles and keep your arms pinned close to your body.

- Don't jerk back on the leash if your dog pulls or lunges. Practice good leash skills and body mechanics.

- Let your dog sniff. Dogs enjoy it! If you try to prevent your dog from sniffing too much, he will more than likely become obsessed with trying to catch any scent that he can.

TEACHING YOUR DOG TO WAIT OR STOP

There is more than one way to teach your dog to wait or stop when outside or while walking on leash. Below are three that work well.

1. Begin walking with your dog by your side (either side is fine — just be consistent when beginning this exercise). Take a few steps with him, and then stop. Remain motionless. When your dog stops, say "Wait" or "Stop," and pause for two to three seconds. Then reward him for waiting or stopping. To prevent him from walking forward,

you can put your palm five to ten inches in front of his nose. When he stops, say "Wait" or "Stop" again. Then pause and treat him.

Dogs tune in to noises and sounds that change frequency. A dog will pay more attention to you when you add inflection to your voice. If you say "Wait" or "Stop" and your dog seems to pay no attention, try a different word, such as "Halt," or an expression such as "Hey" or "Eh," or say the word with more intonation.

When your dog regularly stops beside you when you stop, say "Wait" or "Stop," put your hand in front of his nose, and take a step past him. Then step back and reward him for stopping. Continue to do this until you can walk a few steps past him without him following you. Always return to him to give him a treat.

2. Walk next to your dog toward a fence or other barrier. When you get to the barrier you will both have to stop. Give your verbal signal for stopping just before you actually do. Give him a treat for stopping immediately after he does so. Teaching him the exercise this way pairs your signal with the behavior of stopping. When you feel that your dog understands your signal, stand next to him and begin to walk toward the barrier again. Before you get to the barrier, give your verbal signal and stop. Reward your dog when he stops. Vary the locations in which you teach him to stop when he will regularly stop on cue.

3. While walking your dog on a leash, say your stop or wait signal just before he gets to the end of the leash. He will naturally stop when he gets to the end of the leash. Do not tug on or jerk the leash. Just stand still for a second. Repeat. Your dog will soon learn to stop before he gets to

the end of the leash on hearing your signal. When he does, give him a jackpot of treats! Be sure to give him your verbal cue *before* he gets to the end of the leash. Otherwise, he will not stop when he hears your signal but when he gets to the end of the leash.

Practice giving your signal when your dog is closer to you. Give him treats for stopping before he gets to the end of the leash. When you are confident that your dog understands your verbal signal, let go of the end of the leash when he walks in front of you; he should stop when he hears your signal. Don't forget to reward him generously!

Chapter Seven

POOCH ETIQUETTE:
POSITIVE INTERACTIONS AT DOG PARKS
AND OTHER PLACES WHERE DOGS
PLAY AND MINGLE

I LOVE DOG PARKS AND ANIMAL-FRIENDLY HOTELS, bed-and-breakfasts, and beaches. You can help ensure that such places remain animal friendly by learning proper etiquette, which can prevent mishaps between your dog and other dogs. It is the owners' responsibility to ensure that their dogs behave appropriately at dog parks and other places where dogs are permitted.

Because new dogs entering a park can become overwhelmed by the number of dogs running over to greet them, do not keep your dog directly in front of the entryway to a park. You can teach him a good recall or to sit or look at you for treats whenever new dogs enter.

Stand up for dogs who are harassed by other dogs. Dogs who are continually pestered or bullied by other dogs can be traumatized by the experience — especially if they are harassed by a group of dogs. Speak to the owners and let them know that they need to interrupt the interactions when dogs get harassed.

If your dog taunts or bullies a dog who wants to be left alone, redirect him to a more appropriate behavior, such as going for a walk or playing with a toy. Take him home if he will not stop harassing the other dog. The instant he begins to bully, subdue, dominate, mount, or pursue the other dog, give him a verbal warning, such as "Hey," "Ah-Ah," or "Enough." This warning will be meaningless to him at first. Try to redirect him to another behavior. If he bullies the other dog again after the warning, say your verbal warning again and give him a time-out by removing him from play and socializing. Leave the area, put him on the leash, have him lie down for a couple of minutes, or leave the park. Your timing is important. You must give your warning instantly when your dog behaves inappropriately. If he listens to your warning and stops bullying, praise him and allow him to continue playing.

Dogs who don't play often or who lack proper social skills need short and frequent positive encounters with other dogs. I call these "meet and greets." As your dog approaches another dog, be very happy and positive. When he sniffs another dog or is sniffed by that dog, praise him heavily. Keep the leash relaxed, and angle your body away from the dogs. Do not hover over them. This will give them space and break any tension they may feel. A happy meet and greet should last no more than ten to ninety seconds. After the dogs say hello to each other, encourage your dog to follow you or look at you. Praise and treat him for having had a positive experience with another dog.

If you position dogs who lack social skills parallel to one another and focus their attention on activities other than direct social interaction, they will eventually become much more social and confident when together. Try taking your dog for a walk or a hike with another dog.

If your dog is shy, don't take him to the park when it is packed with dogs. Usually shy dogs like to meet new dogs one at a time or in very small groups. If your dog is shy and you want him to go to a park, use the park during off-hours or when you know there will be a few well-mannered dogs playing. Large groups are too scary for shy dogs. The best dogs for shy dogs to meet are other shy dogs, older dogs, and dogs who are more interested in other activities, such as playing with a ball or sniffing.

PREDICTING AND BREAKING UP DOG FIGHTS

It is not hard to predict a dog fight — especially if you learn how to read canine body language. Dogs raise and tap their paws on the ground and make play-bows when they play positively together.

FIGURE 67. Paw taps and play-bows are frequent ways to initiate play. Notice that the dogs are at a perpendicular angle, or "T," to each other.

They will also regularly change positions and take turns being the offender and defender. If a dog is playing, he will chase another dog or bark or lunge at him but then will run away and/or change his body position.

Changes in the intensity of a dog's growl may indicate that a fight is starting. When dogs play, however, there is no noticeable difference between the sound of a play growl and a real growl. You have to observe how the dogs are interacting with one another. If growling starts and intensifies without stopping, interrupt the play and let the dogs take a break.

FIGURE 68. When socializing, dogs will angle themselves to each other to keep interactions friendly.

Any continual repetitive behavior a dog exhibits, such as excessive pawing, humping, or mounting, may start a fight. The dog on the receiving end of these behaviors may become aggravated or frightened. A fight may also ensue if one dog continuously pursues another. Let dogs take a break from each other if any of these situations occur.

If two dogs are standing on their hind legs or making a lot of face-to-face contact without changing position, a fight may be looming. Distract the dogs from each other and positively inter-rupt the play. Remain calm, and get the dogs focused on another activity.

If a fight breaks out, take the following steps. Your approach will vary depending on the nature of the dogs and the intensity of the fight.

Make a very loud noise. If you are outside near a car, you can try honking the car horn, or if you are inside a house or an apart-ment, ring the doorbell. This may interrupt the fight and give peo-ple enough time to secure each dog.

Pull the aggressor's tail, or remove dogs from each other by pulling up on their hips by the groin. Do *not* pull dogs by their legs, since this can seriously injure them.

If you have access to a water hose, spray water in the direction of the dogs' faces, especially the aggressor's. This will interrupt a fight. Immediately secure each dog. Since the area may be wet, be very careful not to slip.

If there is no one to assist you in interrupting a fight, you can loop a leash under the hips of the more aggressive dog. Lift up on the leash as you walk backward. The dog will be distracted from the fight. Then secure the leash to something stationary, such as a tree, fence, or post. Do the same for the other dog if that dog con-tinues to aggress.

If you have a "bully" breed, such as an American Stafford-shire terrier or American bulldog, it is wise to get a "break stick" (also called a "breaking stick"). These are actually paraphernalia used in dog fighting. A break stick looks like a door wedge with a soft handle. During a fight, bully breeds can hold on to another dog with their jaws. (Many terriers also have this trait, including Jack Russells.) With a break stick you can open a dog's mouth without injuring the dog. Since break sticks are associated with

dog fighting, please be sure to order the sticks through Pit Bull
Rescue Central, at www.pbrc.net/breaksticks.html. A break stick
is not recommended for all dogs. Read the instructions carefully
before using a break stick.

Prevention and anticipation are the best ways to deal with
fights. If a fight does occur, determine what caused it and then prevent those triggers from taking place again. If the dogs were fighting over toys, remove toys before the dogs play and don't bring
toys to the dog park. If one dog simply dislikes the other, try to
go to the park at times when the other dog is not around. Keep
plenty of distance between dogs who do not like each other. This
way dogs who dislike each other still have the opportunity to play
with other dogs but do not have to interact with each other.

There is not much you can do after a fight has occurred. Reprimanding, punishing, or ostracizing your dog after he gets into a
fight is not very helpful. Not only will you fail to resolve any behavioral problems, but you will exacerbate the situation by making
him dislike the other dog even more. Instead, direct your dog to
another activity and remain calm. If you are angry at your dog,
ignore him or take a short break from him. If he was attacked,
don't baby him; act happy or calm, and give him a lot of treats. If
you become too upset, he will become even more upset. If you act
positive and relaxed, he will recover more quickly. Of course,
if your dog was injured in any way, take him to the veterinarian
immediately.

You can also deal with fights preventively by counterconditioning your dog to your grabbing his collar. Then, if he gets in a
fight, his aggression can be redirected in a positive manner to the
person who grabs his collar. By periodically touching and grabbing his collar or harness and giving him a treat or other reward,
you can condition him to anticipate a reward whenever his collar

is grabbed. If a fight breaks out and you grab his collar, he will be more inclined to look at you, as opposed to biting you or continuing to lunge at the other dog.

Please be aware that there is no foolproof way to prevent being bitten if, or when, you interrupt a dog fight. Use common sense to prevent injury to yourself and others if you find yourself having to separate two or more dogs who are fighting. In dog parks or other places where dogs congregate, reward your dog for good behavior and, if he is shy, for socializing. But if he guards you or is protective of his treats, do not give him treats when other dogs are close by.

SUMMARY

Pooch Etiquette

- Keep your dog from hounding other dogs at the entryway to a park. Teach him a good recall or to sit or look at you for a treat when new dogs enter.
- Do not let your dog continually pester a shy dog. Do not allow any dog to bully or harass another.
- If your dog is the bully, redirect him to more appropriate behaviors, such as going for a walk or playing with a toy. Take your dog home if he will not stop harassing another dog.
- Dogs who don't play frequently or who lack social skills need short and frequent positive encounters with other dogs. I call these "meet and greets."
- Large groups are too scary for shy dogs. The best dogs for shy dogs to meet are other shy dogs. Walk shy dogs together to help get them acclimated to each other.

- If growling intensifies during play, give the dogs a time-out or needed break.
- Any continual repetitive behavior a dog exhibits, such as excessive pawing, humping, or mounting, may indicate that a fight is about to occur.
- A fight may break out if your dog constantly pursues a dog who is trying to get away.
- If two dogs remain standing on their hind legs while facing each other, positively interrupt the play and redirect them to other behaviors.
- When dogs play together, they will frequently position themselves next to or at a perpendicular angle to one another, and there will be a lot of paw-raises, play-bows, and changes in body positions.
- Understanding warning signs and interrupting play before it gets out of control are the best ways to prevent dog fights.
- There is no foolproof way to prevent injury when interrupting a dog fight.

Chapter Eight

HOW TO CHOOSE A HUMANE TRAINER

IF YOU ARE LOOKING FOR A TRAINER, it is very important that you find one who embraces humane methodology. Whether the trainer or behaviorist is referred by a veterinarian, groomer, or another behaviorist or you find her in the phone book, you should ask a few questions before hiring. Years of experience are not nearly as important as the methods and philosophy the trainer embraces.

Ask the trainer what equipment she uses or recommends for teaching a dog. A more positively oriented trainer will mention food rewards, play, treats, or a clicker. The trainer should use a flat nylon or fabric collar and harness or a martingale-style collar and a flat leash. A positively oriented trainer will not use nylon slip, choke, chain, pinch, prong, or shock collars.

Ask what a trainer does when dogs bark at each other in class. If she yells at or jerks dogs, or squirts water on dogs for barking, or recommends that you do so, find another trainer.

Avoid trainers whose philosophies involve dominance or who

talk about teaching dogs that you are the "alpha" or "boss" over them, as well as trainers who label dogs stubborn or otherwise indicate that dog training is based on reprimands and punishment.

A polished, skilled, humane trainer will mention positive reinforcement, canine learning, rewards, ignoring unwanted behaviors, increasing the distance between dogs who are barking, and encouraging dogs to focus on you or to perform other behaviors if they are exhibiting behaviors that you don't like.

Avoid trainers who suggest a quick fix to a problem that you have barely explained. If you have a dog with a behavioral problem stemming from aggression, anxiety, or fear, a more skilled and positively oriented trainer will want to spend a few hours with you so that she can understand the problem. The trainer or behaviorist will ask you questions and may even ask you to fill out questionnaires, screens, or other paperwork elaborating on problem behaviors and/or other concerns you may have about your dog. This information provides valuable insights so the trainer or behaviorist can better assess how to best improve and resolve the situation for you and your dog.

Be wary of crossover trainers, or trainers who promote positive training on paper or in advertisements but actually fall back on bully training or what is frequently called "yank and praise" or "jerk and praise." These trainers might initially promote positive reinforcement, simply because they throw food into the equation, but when a problem arises that they can't resolve, they resort to tactics such as kneeing a dog in the chest for jumping or squirting him with a water bottle for barking. A humane trainer will not use the leash as the primary means of control and will not encourage you to yank or jerk on your dog's collar to elicit a behavior.

Finally, watch how your dog responds to a trainer. If your dog is fearful or unusually hesitant or seems to dislike the trainer, you will likely do better with a different trainer. If a trainer overly criticizes or seems annoyed or frustrated by your dog or you feel in any way uncomfortable with how the trainer or behaviorist interacts with your dog, don't hesitate to find another.

Your dog should feel happy and safe with the trainer. If your dog has any fear or aggression issues, a good trainer or behaviorist will not do anything to purposely solicit, instigate, or encourage your dog's fearfulness or aggression. She will not intentionally frighten your dog or intensify his fears. If any trainer becomes in any way physically abusive, run — don't walk — away. Find a trainer or behaviorist who will treat your dog humanely.

A few organizations can be helpful when you're looking for a trainer or behaviorist: the Association of Pet Dog Trainers, the Animal Behavior Society, and the Association of Animal Behavior Professionals. However, membership in these associations does not ensure that a trainer will abide by their philosophies. Even if a trainer is certified by or affiliated with a professional association, be sure that she uses positive and reputable training techniques.

SUMMARY

How to Choose a Humane Trainer

- Years of experience are not as important as the methods and philosophies a trainer embraces.
- A skilled humane trainer will mention positive reinforcement, canine learning, rewards, and ignoring unwanted behaviors. She will use food, play, and other rewards to teach dogs. A humane trainer will not use nylon slip,

choke, chain, pinch, prong, or shock collars. She will use a flat nylon or fabric collar and harness or a martingale-style collar and a flat leash. She will not use the leash as the primary way to control your dog, nor will she advocate yanking or jerking the leash to elicit a behavior.

- If you feel in any way uncomfortable with a trainer or feel she is abusive, find another one.
- Your dog should feel safe and happy with the trainer.
- Avoid trainers who bully, scruff, poke, nudge, or hit dogs or who promote an "alpha" mentality over dogs, as well as trainers who squirt dogs with water, label dogs stubborn, or otherwise indicate that they use a training system based on punishment and corrections. These trainers make dogs work through intimidation.
- If your dog has fear or aggression issues, a good trainer or behaviorist will not instigate or intensify his fearfulness or aggression. A humane trainer will not intentionally frighten your dog.
- Look for trainers and behaviorists who belong to professional associations, such as the Association of Pet Dog Trainers, the Animal Behavior Society, and the Association of Animal Behavior Professionals. Be aware that trainers and behaviorists do not have to abide by the philosophies of the organizations in order to be members.
- Hire a humane trainer or behaviorist who uses kind and nonviolent methods. Your dog will be thankful and happy you did.

Summary

THE PRINCIPLES OF THIS BOOK

- Use positive techniques to teach dogs.
- Always reward and acknowledge your dog for exhibiting desired behavior.
- Don't wait for your dog to exhibit a behavior that you don't like before you reinforce a behavior that you do.
- Never expose your dog to stressors in a way that will upset him. Set him up for success.
- Pair anything that frightens your dog with experiences that he enjoys.
- Do not yank or jerk your dog on the leash — especially when he is around other dogs or people.
- Do not punish your dog for urinating or defecating in the house. Use proper housetraining methods.
- Don't reprimand your dog for growling, lunging, or being upset.
- Desensitize and countercondition your dog to things that make him anxious or frighten him.

- Teach your dog easy and alternate behaviors to perform in situations in which he feels unsure or uncomfortable.
- Get your dog a toy bin and encourage him to play with his toys.
- Learn good leash techniques.
- Hire a humane, positive trainer to help you to teach your dog.
- Always position your body at an angle to dogs. Stand or kneel next to or at a perpendicular angle to them.
- Pet your dog on his neck and chest and under his chin — not directly on top of his head.
- Do not stare down a dog. It does not establish dominance, and will simply make a dog fearful of you.
- Pivot away from your dog and stop making eye contact with him if he gets too hyper and jumps on you. Give him attention when he is calm.
- Don't focus on your dog's unwanted behaviors. If you keep focusing on behaviors you dislike, you will spend less time reinforcing the behaviors you want.
- Dogs love to learn! Teaching your dog should be fun.

Appendix One

INTRODUCING DOGS AND CATS
TO EACH OTHER

IT CAN TAKE TIME FOR DOGS AND CATS who have never met to acclimate to each other, but many dogs and cats can coexist peacefully and happily together, and great friendships can develop between them. Some dogs are very gentle with kitties and actually prefer the company of cats to that of other dogs. Some dogs need training to be around kitties. Other dogs need strict management.

Unfortunately, when people introduce dogs to cats, the usual scenario is that the dog chases the cat, and the cat ends up hiding in the basement or closet or under the bed. This is unnecessary and not fair to either animal — especially your kitty. Your cat should not be relegated to the basement or bedroom. Below are some helpful guidelines and suggestions to follow to introduce a dog and cat to each other.

If you have a dog who is shy, fearful, or timid and a kitty who is territorial, confident, or aggressive, reverse some of these suggestions. Interrupt and prevent your kitty from being aggressive to your dog, and reward your dog for showing calm, confident behavior around your cat. Reward your cat for being friendly to your dog or for ignoring him.

Cats love kindness and positive reinforcement and are very amenable to behavior modification too.

FIGURE 69. Dogs and cats can live nicely together.

Designate a room or location in the house that is entirely your cat's territory. Teach your dog that he is not allowed in this area.

Your dog should not have access to litter boxes or to your cat's food. In addition, your cat should not have to pass or dodge your dog to get to food and water bowls or litter pans.

Make sure your kitty has extra territory and places to go to feel safe and to get away from your dog. Invest in a few good cat trees or cat condos. These add vertical territory for your cat and will make your kitty feel safer around your dog.

Use Feliway (a synthetic pheromone) plug-ins to calm and soothe your kitty.

If you frequently wear a perfume, cologne, or lotion, rub it on your skin. When it dries, pet your animals. This way you can create a "communal" odor. Scent is very important to animals. If your dog and kitty smell similar to you and to each other, they may bond more quickly.

Let your dog and cat get used to each other's smells through a closed door. Reward your dog for showing calm behavior. Treat and feed your kitty when your dog is nearby. When your dog is calm and mild-mannered around your cat, your cat will be relaxed around your dog.

Be sure to give your kitty plenty of attention

Exercise your dog before introducing him to your cat. If your dog has just run a few miles or played ball in the park for an hour, he will be calmer, less energetic, and more relaxed around your cat. Do not introduce your dog to your cat if your dog has not had any exercise.

Feed your cat and dog at the same time so they can see each other. If your cat is afraid of your dog, feed them in separate rooms. This establishes a positive association between them and gives them a reason to like each other.

Always place your kitty on higher surfaces than your dog. This protects your cat and makes him feel more confident. If your kitty is less likely to run, your dog will be less likely to chase.

Introduce your cat to your dog when your dog is tired, resting, or sleeping. While your dog is sleeping or resting, feed your cat treats on the cat condo or sofa, or pet and brush your kitty on your lap. Do not bring your cat over to your dog or force or push an interaction.

Reward your dog for ignoring your cat, and if possible, for lying down and relaxing. This is a good time to provide your dog with a chew toy, treat ball, or other food-dispensing toy. If your dog cannot relax, teach your dog to back away, or temporarily remove your dog from the room. Then allow your dog back into the room and reward him for being calm, friendly and relaxed, and for ignoring your cat.

Teach your dog polite manners. Train your dog using positive reinforcement when your cat is in the room. This will teach your dog how to behave and to listen to you when your cat is present.

Use a front-clip body harness or head halter when introducing your dog to your cat, and make sure to have your dog on a leash. This will give you more control. It will prevent your dog from chasing your cat and will allow you to reward him for behaving gently around your kitty. Keep the leash relaxed and practice good leash skills. Reward your dog any time he looks away from your cat.

Give your dog and cat reasons to like each other. Feed them extra-good food and treats when they see each other. Prevent any negative interactions or altercations from occurring, and manage the environment so that your dog can be rewarded for showing friendly, nonthreatening behaviors.

Play with your dog quietly when your kitty is in the room. If your dog does not chase or pursue your cat, he should be given a fantastic reward.

Prevent your dog from chasing your cat by immediately interrupting your dog and redirecting him to a more appropriate behavior, such as coming to you, chewing on a toy, or lying down.

If your dog barks at your cat, remove him from the room. Bring him back in and reward him for being calm, friendly, and gentle, or for ignoring your cat.

When you are not there to supervise, your dog and cat should be separated until you know they will behave well with each other.

If your dog still cannot be trusted around your cat after you have followed the above suggestions, seek the help of a qualified humane dog trainer or animal behaviorist. Your dog may need to be fully managed or supervised around your kitty, or completely separated from your cat.

Appendix Two

LIVING WITH MORE THAN ONE DOG

LIVING WITH MORE THAN ONE DOG can be a rewarding experience. Dogs love the company of other dogs. Knowing how to prevent problems and teaching dogs how to share resources so they do not bully each other, or pester you, is pivotal to having a harmonious multidog home. If you regularly let your dogs work it out among themselves, you give them a clear signal that you do not want to be involved when there is social conflict. If there is then an emergency, and you need to get your dogs' attention, they will be less likely to look to you for guidance.

Dogs will frequently fight or compete over resources. Resources include your attention, eye contact, affection, and praise; locations in the house and in the car; toys, balls, bones, food, and beds. A little preparedness on your part can go a long way toward preventing conflict. Your dogs should wait their turns for affection and food, respond to their names, and know how to sit, stay, look at you, and leave or drop objects.

Teach your dogs that all toys, affection, games, play, and petting come from you only when they are nice to each other. If they mis-behave or bully each other for resources and your attention, give them a time-out or remove what triggered the behavior. Make sure the situation is managed so the problem does not reoccur.

FIGURES 70, 71, 72. Teaching dogs together will reward polite manners.

Provide plenty of resources for your dogs so that there is little competition between them. If you have only one food bowl, dog toy, or dog bed, your dogs will be forced to take turns or fight over them.

Say your dogs' names routinely so each dog can figure out who is being focused on. If other dogs get involved when you are focusing on an individual, turn your back on the others or look away from them.

Do not give your dogs attention for being nudgy, barking at you, jumping on you, or bullying each other. Don't pet your dogs when they barricade you or push themselves on you. Teach your dogs impulse control, and reward polite manners.

All dogs should wait for treats and meals or have places to go when they eat so that they do not intrude on each other.

Dogs should wait or be taught to sit before they go outside. Please do not ask an older dog to sit; older dogs frequently have hip and knee problems, and sitting can be painful for them. Ask older dogs to wait or stay instead. The goal is not for your dogs to sit, but for them to not barge through doors when you open them. If you have a young dog who regularly hesitates when you ask him to sit, take him to a veterinarian.

When you pet one dog and another dog intrudes so that he becomes the center of attention, if you reward him you are rewarding that behavior. The dogs then compete for your attention, and one dog will inevitably be driven away. This does not set a good precedent for you as a leader.

If you are petting a dog and another dog barges in and pushes that dog away, ignore the dog who intruded by looking away or turning your back to him. Continue petting the first dog. If the other dog begins to nudge or growl at the dog who is receiving attention from you, stand up and look away from both dogs. When the dog who growled or nudged his way in sees that his behavior did not work for him and loses interest, go back and pet the dog you had been giving attention to.

If dogs growl at each other over an object or a bone, remove it. If a dog has a toy or other object and another dog intimidates him by staring at him, interrupt the stare and direct that dog to another behavior. If one dog takes a toy or an object from another dog or makes that dog drop the object or leave the area, remove the item from the dog who took it and give it back to the dog who originally had it. You may have to do this multiple times, but your dogs will get a message from you: bullying behavior doesn't work. You will notice a remarkable change in your dogs' behaviors. The dog who may be regularly harassed or bullied will thank you, and there should be less conflict between the dogs in the future.

If there is confrontation in the home that has turned into fights, please see a professional humane dog trainer or animal behaviorist for help. Reread chapters 5 and 8 to help you.

Appendix Three

DEAF DOGS

ALL THE EXERCISES IN THIS BOOK can be used or modified to teach deaf dogs.

The best ways to teach a deaf dog are to use hand signals and positive reinforcement and to acclimate him to a routine. To learn sign language online, visit www.handspeak.com.

Give your dog a vibrating/chime collar. You can teach him to pay attention to you when the collar vibrates through the attention exercises (see page 32), and the vibration can replace calling him by his name to get his attention.

Teach your dog two hand signals: one for "Good" and another for "Great." The hand signal for good should mean one or a few treats or small rewards. The signal for great should mean many treats or a highly desirable reward.

You will also need to teach your dog a visual release signal to let him know when you no longer have expectations of him.

Deaf dogs should only be allowed off-leash in a secure or fenced-in area.

Deaf dogs can be startled by sudden touches or by being unexpectedly wakened. Desensitize and countercondition your dog to being touched. Touch his shoulder and give him a treat, or put your hand in front of his nose to let your smell wake him. Give him a treat and/or lots of affection every time you wake him up or startle him. Read chapter 5 for more information on desensitization and counterconditioning.

Similarly, desensitize and countercondition your dog to having his collar grabbed. Every time you touch his collar, make sure that something good happens to him.

Some websites to help you address the needs of deaf dogs are www.deafdogs.org, www.handicappedpets.com, and www.special needspets.com

Appendix Four

SAMPLE BEHAVIOR MODIFICATION PLANS: ARI'S AND ZEE'S STORIES

BY PROVIDING THESE STORIES, I hope to teach people how to apply behavior modification principles to real-life situations. Often it is difficult for us to apply theory to practice. All the techniques taught in this book can be applied to dogs who are suffering from issues such as fear and anxiety. All dogs love to learn when taught in a positive way. And all dogs — as well as other animals — trust, once they are treated nicely. I hope that by sharing Ari's and Zee's stories, I will help you embrace compassionate techniques when teaching your dog.

ARI'S STORY
(SAMPLE BEHAVIOR MODIFICATION PLAN)
Statement by Nancy Bersani, Milton Animal League

In June 2005, the Milton Animal Shelter received a call from another shelter regarding a puppy who was being returned for aggression and dominance. The family returning the puppy thought she should be euthanized.

Ari was a mixed-breed puppy born on a small farm in March of that year. A woman driving by the farm saw a sign advertising puppies for sale. Ari was the only puppy in the litter that could be coaxed out from a hole underneath the shed where the puppies were living. The woman did not see the puppies' mother or father and was given no information about them. At the time, Ari was approximately six weeks old and infested with ticks. The woman's landlord did not allow pets, and after he discovered that Ari was living in the house the woman gave the puppy to the shelter.

The same day that Ari was surrendered to the shelter she was adopted by a family with two teenagers. After ten days Ari was returned to the shelter again. The family called the shelter and said that they were bringing her back because of her aggressiveness. They felt that Ari should be killed. Ari was now four months old. The shelter staff did not want to kill a four-month-old puppy, so they convinced the family to bring Ari to the Milton Animal League, a no-kill shelter.

Ari was an active puppy whose reaction to any touch was to quickly put her mouth on you, leaving bite marks and tearing clothing. The family stated that any physical correction (such as grabbing her collar and shaking it) resulted in a bite from Ari. If the person then shook the collar harder, Ari would respond by biting harder. When I took Ari outside to our fenced exercise pen she would run around the perimeter and then head straight toward me, jumping up on me (or anyone else within reach), grabbing clothes, skin, or hair in her teeth and leaving marks and drawing blood. Leashing her was a battle and initially took two people — one to distract her, and one to put on the leash. Ari would also chew everything in the shelter, including walls and doorways. I tried Bitter Apple spray, but she seemed to like it and licked it off!

A local behaviorist was working with Ari. She called Ari

dominant and used harsh corrections and punitive techniques. Ari's behavior became worse. We finally asked this woman to stop working with Ari. I instinctively felt that punishment was not the right approach. Because of Ari's behavior, I was the only person at the shelter who would work with her. A former MSPCA law enforcement officer began volunteering and took Ari for long hikes once a week. Ari looked forward to these outings, but she would always revert to biting and jumping on people, including the volunteer. No one thought she was adoptable.

We had heard about Alana Stevenson, and I called her. She agreed to work with Ari and to set up a behavior modification plan for volunteers at the shelter to follow. Alana set up a positive, reward-based program for Ari that was to be followed by every volunteer who worked with her. Alana said that if people could not follow the recommended techniques then they should not be allowed to interact with Ari.

I started using the positive training methods Alana suggested. I began giving Ari treats for appropriate behavior and ignoring her for inappropriate behaviors. I walked Ari twice a day and threw toys for her in the exercise pen as long as she was behaving. I gave Ari treats for letting me touch parts of her body without biting me. Ari improved daily and could be worked with by anyone who followed Alana's recommendations. I continued with Ari, and she improved so much that she rarely put her mouth on me. Since she was biting me hard enough to draw blood when she arrived at the shelter, this was a great improvement! People commented on Ari's improved behavior. In February 2006, after Ari had been at the shelter for eight months, a young couple adopted her. They followed our behavior modification recommendations. Ari has done remarkably well in her new home. People have complimented the couple on how well behaved Ari is.

Her new family is committed to continuing her training and only uses positive methods. Ari is great with everyone, including children. Ari is such a wonderful success story for our shelter!

MY BEHAVIOR MODIFICATION PLAN

Nancy called me and told me that Milton Animal League had been given a puppy from another shelter because the puppy was aggressive. The shelter volunteers thought that she was dominant. It had been recommended that she be euthanized since she was considered unadoptable. When she bit people, she punctured skin. I was told that a trainer had been working with her and considered her a very strong-willed and stubborn dog. I asked what kind of collar the trainer was using and was told the trainer was relying on a choke collar. I agreed to see Ari and to set up a behavior modification plan for the shelter staff and other volunteers to follow. I knew that a four-month-old puppy wasn't trying to be dominant, and I had my suspicions as to what her problems were and how people were reinforcing them.

When I first saw Ari at the shelter, she used her mouth a lot when people touched her. Although I had been told that Ari was out of control when play-biting, it was clear to me that when Ari bit people she wasn't play-biting at all. Nor was she as aggressive or stubborn as her former family, the previous shelter, and the prior trainer had thought.

When I saw Ari interact with people it was clear to me that she did not understand how to respond to touch. She was sensitive to human body language and very reactive when people leaned over her or reached their hands toward her head or face. Based on the red marks, nicks, and scratches on Nancy's and other volunteers' arms, I could tell that Ari didn't have good bite inhibition. This wasn't at all surprising, since she was only six weeks old when she was rescued. Ari's puppyhood lacked socialization, play with other puppies, proper chewing outlets, and any human consistency. Instead of taking the time to teach Ari how to play appropriately, her caretakers had reprimanded her for both playing and chewing. When Ari had experienced difficulty with being touched or handled, she had been reprimanded yet again. Since she had been passed around from shelter to shelter and from person to person, she had little understanding of what humans expected from her.

Being a social animal, Ari was desperate for attention. She wanted to interact with both people and dogs. However, since Ari was very intense and reactive with people, people were very punitive and reactive to her in return. This was not a good start for a puppy.

Ari also jumped on people, pulled on the leash, and frantically barked and lunged at other dogs in the kennel. She walked by dogs who barked frenetically at her and so she growled and barked at them in return. All the dogs in the kennel were stressed.

I volunteered to work with Ari for a few hours and took her for a hike in the woods. When I interacted with Ari out of the shelter environment, I was able to observe her likes and dislikes. I quickly discovered that Ari loved swimming and was very bright and curious. I also saw that she definitely enjoyed having company. She seemed to like both men and women, which was good because it increased her chances of adoption. We passed by a small group of people, and someone came over to pet Ari. I told the woman to stand next to Ari and to only pet her as I was treating Ari. Ari did very well. She did not jump on the woman or try to bite her. I allowed the interaction to continue for just a minute, and then I redirected Ari to follow and walk with me.

Ari bit whenever she wanted something. If we dawdled on the trail, she jumped and attacked my legs. She bit my hands when I held or restrained her. And when she bit, it really did hurt. When I brought Ari back to the shelter, I gave Nancy a behavior modification plan for volunteers to follow when working with Ari. My recommendations were as follows:

No one was to use punitive techniques or reprimands when working with Ari. She was not to be walked on a choke collar or be pushed down for jumping. She was not to be yelled at, and no one was to grab her muzzle when she bit or to tell her "No" when they disliked her behavior. These approaches had already failed to teach Ari how to behave and made interacting with people even more difficult for her.

I recommended that Ari be walked with a Sense-ation Harness. If she jumped on anyone, that person was to pivot away from her, break eye contact, and ignore her. If Ari was relentless, the person was to remain motionless and wait it out or leave, but under no circumstances was anyone to interact with her or reprimand her for jumping. Any time anyone touched her collar or any part of her body, she was to be given a treat; the yummier the treat, the better. When Ari seemed receptive to being touched and having her collar gently held, people could pet her and/or hold on to her collar for longer periods of time before giving her treats. I recommended that volunteers give Ari treats for any eye contact and attention she gave them when they walked her. Any time that she did not pull on the leash they were to praise her and reward her with play, food, and games.

Everyone was to stand or kneel parallel to or at a perpendicular angle to Ari. People were to always position their bodies at a slight angle to hers. No one was to approach her from the front, lean over her, or pet her directly on top of her head. If anyone wanted to pet Ari, this person was to be instructed to pet her under her chin and on her chest. People were only to interact with her when she was not biting or jumping.

I recommended that Ari be given treats whenever she walked quietly by other dogs in the kennels. In addition, people could reward her for eye contact. The goal was for her to walk to her kennel — without barking at the other dogs — to get a special treat.

I also recommended that Ari be walked with other dogs. When she felt comfortable, she was to be allowed to play with other dogs in the exercise/play area of the shelter. It was crucial for her to have positive social interactions with other dogs. Finally, I advised that any follow-up training for Ari should come from a trainer who used only positive, reward-based methods.

A few weeks after Nancy implemented my recommendations, I was told that Ari had greatly improved. Because Nancy embraced humane, positive training, Ari was given a wonderful opportunity to have a nice life with a family who cares for her.

Every day I see many wonderful dogs whose potential could be realized if only people would take a step back and consider the dogs' needs. Unfortunately, our relationships with dogs are often based on misunderstandings and ignorance. When people use compassionate training techniques, a beautiful partnership grows between humans and dogs. Our relationships with dogs can be based on love, respect, and friendship — not dominance, control, and obedience.

ZEE'S STORY
(SAMPLE BEHAVIOR MODIFICATION PLAN)

Statement by Annette Kaplovsky, Zee's owner

I am Zee's third home. As I understand it, after doing some research, as a puppy he lived with a bunch of children and another dog in his first home. The mother of the household became pregnant again and did not want two dogs. The family gave Zee to the city pound run by animal control. At the shelter, it was noted that he was a friendly Labrador puppy. He was then given to a couple who told shelter staff that they had euthanized their previous dog for aggression. Eleven months later they returned Zee to the shelter with a muzzle on him. The couple said that Zee was aggressive too. Zee was at the shelter for four months before I met him.

I was looking for a yellow Lab and wanted to rescue one. A friend found Zee (his name was "Cesar" at the time) on PetFinder. I met him, and fell in love with him instantly. The shelter staff was nervous about me adopting Zee. Zee lunged at people in the kennels when they approached him. On leash, he would lunge at people if they looked at him or tried to pet him. The lead volunteer remembered how good-natured Zee was at the shelter as a puppy before the second adoption. She wanted to give Zee another opportunity and a better chance. She told me about Alana Stevenson and that she could help Zee overcome his difficult past and help me to heal him emotionally.

When I first adopted Zee, he lunged at people if they looked directly at him. He lunged at people if they went to pet him or approach him. Because I was unsure what to do and did not want to put Zee at risk, I kept Zee at home, and we went for brief car rides together.

I contacted Alana and started working with her. I had taken many dog-training classes and seminars with my past dogs and was familiar with positive training in an informal way. None of these classes or seminars taught me how to work with dogs in realistic situations. All training was based on teaching a dog to perform in an obedience ring. What Alana taught me was beyond anything I had learned. The techniques she taught me worked immediately. Zee was very excited to learn from me and loved going to her training classes.

I used the desensitization techniques Alana recommended. I began walking Zee at a deserted ice-skating rink, where there was very little foot traffic. When he would see a stranger in the distance, I treated him. I kept Zee at a distance so that he would feel safe. I knew we were making progress when one day we passed two men on motorcycles in full regalia racing their engines. I put myself between them and Zee and treated him continuously. He passed them without being fearful, reacting, or lunging.

Zee made great progress as we continued attending Alana's classes. Alana told students to greet Zee by saying hello to him while I treated him. People were receptive and friendly to him, and he began taking treats from the people in class. I then began walking him in places where he would see and meet more people. I introduced him to my friends. I instructed them to angle away from him when they greeted him. I gave him treats and praised him when people greeted him. After I worked with him in this way, he began to enjoy meeting people.

When I first adopted Zee, he didn't know how to play. Having had Labs in the past, I knew they loved retrieving and swimming. Using what I learned in Alana's classes, I taught Zee how to fetch and retrieve. He now loves to play ball, and we play it daily. With Alana's encouragement, I took him swimming, and of course he's a natural. I have had Zee now for four and a half years. He has fabulous doggy friends. Children can approach him, strangers can pet him, and he meets people happily. He always has a smile on his face.

Every time I look at him, I am in awe at his progress. He has gone from being a dog who was worried, hesitant, and fearful — therefore feeling the need to defend himself by being reactive —

to being a dog who is happy and trusts people. I am so thankful that I met Alana and could make Zee's world a better place.

MY BEHAVIOR MODIFICATION PLAN

I met Zee after I was called by a shelter volunteer. She told me that Zee (named "Cesar" at the time) was aggressive and lunged at people when they would look at him in the kennel. When he was outside on leash, Zee lunged at anyone who looked at him or approached to pet him. The volunteer said he had been adopted by people who earlier had a dog euthanized for aggression. She had known Zee when he was at the shelter before this second adoption. He was a happy Lab puppy then. But he was returned to the shelter after this second adoption for being "aggressive."

I met Zee in front of the shelter, and when I said hello he was not aggressive to me. The volunteer rolled her eyes and said, "I told everyone he'd like Alana and won't show his behaviors in front of her." Because Zee was very receptive to my signals of friendliness and nonaggression, and because of the additional information the volunteer had given me, I knew Zee's behaviors were due to how people had treated him. I had no doubt he would blossom with kindness, positive training, and counterconditioning. I suggested Zee attend my classes if a volunteer wanted to bring him.

When Zee first came to my training class with the volunteer, he was visibly anxious, worried, and withdrawn. He avoided eye contact. Zee showed no signs of aggression to dogs or people in class. It was at this time I met Annette. She wanted to adopt Zee, so she came to observe him.

Once Annette adopted Zee, she brought him regularly to my training classes. We focused heavily on attention work, which counterconditioned him to eye contact and taught him to take cues from Annette. I instructed Annette to give Zee treats any time he looked at a person or dog in class.

In classes, I teach "meet and greets," which are a great way to introduce dogs to each other without putting pressure on them. Zee never showed signs of aggression to dogs in training class or at the shelter. He was very friendly to dogs and had great appeasement gestures. Due to his reactivity to people, Annette and shelter volunteers were worried about how he would behave toward dogs. I eased Annette's fears so that Zee could play and socialize with dogs in class both on- and off-leash. Zee made great friends in training class. Because Zee greeted dogs in a friendly and nonconfrontational way, he helped timid dogs socialize in classes as well. He then met these dogs for play dates outside of class, which helped him to meet and socialize with people (the dogs owners) in a safe and positive way.

To address his hesitation when meeting people, I asked students to give Zee treats when he approached. When he was relaxed and comfortable approaching people, I instructed them to approach Zee and to reward him for making eye contact. Since he was happy in class and it was a safe place for him, he warmed up to people in classes immediately. When Zee was comfortable making eye contact, I allowed students to pet him. All students in class knew safe, friendly, and proper body language when greeting dogs. No one approached Zee directly, pet him on his head, or leaned over him. Annette praised and treated Zee during and after these friendly greetings and interactions with people. Zee was never pushed into situations that he couldn't handle or that were stressful to him. Zee progressed to the next level only when he was happy and ready to do so.

Zee attended five class sessions. Each session was six weeks. He learned how to come to Annette when she called him, to walk on a relaxed leash, to make eye contact with her, to lie down, to wait, to stay, and to interact with people and dogs in fun and positive ways. Since training was based on play and rewards, Zee felt safe in class and loved to learn. Since classes were taught in a park, it made behaviors Zee learned easily transferable to other outdoor locations. The more classes Zee attended, the happier and more excited he became when meeting people and dogs. Annette used the techniques she learned in classes and applied them to her and Zee's daily life.

When I first met Zee he was worried and clearly anxious of what people might do to him. He needed safety, guidance, benevolent leadership, and a caring owner. Annette provided these for him. Zee is a very happy dog now and is enthusiastic about life. He adores Annette, plays ball regularly, and loves swimming. Through kindness and humane training, Zee's trust and faith in people was restored.

Appendix Five

HARMFUL TRAINING TECHNIQUES

NUMEROUS HARMFUL TRAINING TECHNIQUES are often used when people teach dogs. The approaches listed below are seldom effective when teaching your dog. These methods can create or intensify fear, reactivity, jumping on people, aggression, mouthiness, and anxiety in your dog. Do not use them.

- Sticking your fingernail into a puppy's tongue to stop play-biting.
- Pushing your puppy's lip into his tooth to stop play-biting.
- Sticking your finger down a dog's throat to stop play-biting.
- Growling in a dog's face. This is an aggressive behavior and will make fearful dogs more fearful and reactive dogs more reactive. The side effects can include increased aggression, anxiety, avoidance of the owner, and fear of eye contact.
- Staring down a dog. Dogs are sensitive to eye contact. Staring down a dog is a direct threat and confrontational.

Forcing a dog to look at you is abusive. Dogs should learn to trust eye contact and your intentions.

- "Alpha rolling" a dog. Pushing your dog onto his back is an inappropriate way to correct a behavior. Dogs do not force other dogs onto their backs into "submission." Dogs will voluntarily roll onto their sides during both play and conflict. The alpha roll is a technique created by people thinking they are behaving like wolves, when neither dogs nor wolves exhibit this behavior. Parental wolves do not alpha roll their offspring.

- Using choke chains and pinch collars. There is no need to inflict pain on your dog by using such collars. Chain collars restrict a dog's breathing and can cause damage to his spine and/or trachea. Pinch collars cause pain and bruising. Excessive use of pinch collars can cause bleeding and scarring. The use of chain collars is condemned by the UK-based Association of Pet Dog Trainers.

- Kneeing a dog in the chest for jumping. Kneeing your dog will not eliminate the behavior — it will usually make jumping worse. Jumping up on people and other dogs is a gesture usually exhibited by puppies, young submissive dogs, and young energetic dogs to seek reassurance and to get attention.

- Stepping on a dog's paws. Stepping on his paws will make jumping worse. It will make your dog anxious and will damage your relationship with him.

- Keeping your dog crated for over four hours a day on a regular basis to manage your dog's environment, instead of teaching him how to behave in the house when left alone.

- Shocking your dog. Shock collars cause pain, make dogs fearful and reactive, and decrease their ability to play and be spontaneous.
- Yelling "No" at your dog when you have failed to teach him what you would like him to do or alternative behaviors.
- Hitting your dog. When you hit your dog, you fail to teach him another way of behaving and will make him fearful of you.
- Shaking a dog by the scruff. This is abusive and will make your dog fear you. Shaking a dog by the scruff repeatedly or shaking a young puppy can cause cognitive damage. It can hinder your dog's ability to learn, decrease his attention span, and make him fearful, anxious, hyperactive, or reactive.

Appendix Six

FOOD AND TREATS

USE VERY SMALL PIECES OF FOOD as treats when training. The pieces should be small enough that your dog will want more when you are done. You can feed your dog meals through training exercises or treat-dispensing toys or use kibble for beginning exercises. Use highly desirable treats when your dog is overstimulated or distracted, when guests are over, or when he is outdoors, frightened, stressed, or anxious. If you haven't fed your dog a variety of foods, add new foods or treats to his diet one at a time. Don't give him too much all at once. If your dog will sit in the living room for kibble or just praise, don't give him anything too valuable or your leftovers from dinner for doing so. He will not want to work for cookies and other treats if he gets his favorite foods just for looking cute.

I tend to stick with less-processed food. Generally, whole foods are better than packaged foods. Avoid giving your dog treats or foods that contain corn meal, corn syrup, artificial colors and preservatives, by-products, rendered animal products, or meat or animal digest. Don't give him heavily processed or neon-colored treats.

I tend to avoid processed liver treats, jerky treats, and freeze-dried lamb, pork, and beef treats. These treats tend to be rich and can cause stomach and intestinal upset if given in large amounts. They also have strong odors and are difficult for many people to work with.

Treats can be vegetables your dog likes. Banana chips, baked or dried fruits and veggies, such as apples or sweet potato chews can make fun treats. Fresh fruit, such as bananas and apples, brown rice, oat cereals, and peanut butter (ground, plain, and unsalted) can be used for training. Your dog can lick peanut butter off a spoon as a reward. You can use high-quality packaged dog food as treats during training, especially for puppies. High-quality dog foods are available at independently owned pet supply stores, health food stores, and grooming shops. These foods usually do not contain corn meal, artificial colors or flavors, by-products, rendered animal products, or meat and animal digest.

Most dogs like carob and molasses treats, which smell really good. I have a lot of success with them. Dogs tend to prefer soft foods over crunchy ones. Crush hard or crunchy cookies into small pieces to make them last longer. Do not feed your dog grapes, raisins, or onions. Never feed your dog chocolate.

Resources

PLEASE CONSIDER ADOPTING AN ANIMAL from a shelter or rescue league. There are millions of animals discarded and abandoned who need loving and lifelong caring homes. Visit your local animal shelter or www.petfinder.com or to find a loving animal in need of adoption.

Spay or neuter your pets. This will prevent the unnecessary overpopulation resulting from unethical breeding practices and neglect. Spaying and neutering will also prevent and resolve many behavioral problems.

There are many books available to help you learn about animal behavior. Here are a few recommendations:

Aloff, Brenda. *Aggression in Dogs: Practical Management, Prevention & Behaviour Modification.* Wenatchee, WA: Dogwise, 2002.

Balcombe, Jonathan. *Pleasurable Kingdom: Animals and the Nature of Feeling Good.* New York: Palgrave MacMillan, 2006.

———. *Second Nature: The Inner Lives of Animals.* New York: Palgrave MacMillan, 2010.

Bekoff, Marc. *The Animal Manifesto: Six Reasons for Expanding Our Compassion Footprint.* Novato, CA: New World Library, 2010.

———. *The Emotional Lives of Animals: A Leading Scientist Explores Animal Joy, Sorrow, and Empathy — and Why They Matter.* Novato, CA: New World Library, 2007.

Bekoff, Marc, and Jessica Pierce. *Wild Justice: The Moral Lives of Animals.* Chicago: University of Chicago Press, 2010.

Campbell, William E. *Behavior Problems in Dogs*, 3d rev. ed. Wenatchee, WA: Dogwise, 1999.

———. *Dog Behavior Problems: The Counselor's Handbook*. Wenatchee, WA: Dogwise, 1999.

Clothier, Suzanne. *Bones Would Rain from the Sky: Deepening Our Relationships with Dogs*. New York: Warner, 2002.

Dennison, Pam. *How to Right a Dog Gone Wrong: A Road Map for Rehabilitating Aggressive Dogs*. Suwanee, GA: Alpine Blue Ribbon Books, 2005.

Dodman, Nicholas. *Dogs Behaving Badly: An A–Z Guide to Understanding and Curing Behavioral Problems in Dogs*. New York, Bantam, 2000.

Donaldson, Jean. *Dogs Are from Neptune*, 2d ed. Wenatchee, WA: Dogwise, 2010.

———. *Mine! A Practical Guide to Resource Guarding in Dogs*. Wenatchee, WA: Dogwise, 2002.

Dunbar, Ian. *How to Teach a New Dog Old Tricks*, 2d ed. Berkeley, CA: James & Kenneth Publishers, 1991.

Fox, Michael, Elizabeth Hodgkins, and Marion E. Smart. *Not Fit for a Dog: The Truth about Manufactured Dog and Cat Food*. Fresno, CA: Quill Driver Books, 2009.

McConnell, Patricia, and Karen B. London. *Feisty Fido: Help for the Leash-Reactive Dog*, 2d ed. Black Earth, WI: McConnell Publishing, 2009.

Miller, Pat. *The Power of Positive Dog Training*. New York: Howell Book House, 2001.

Overall, Karen. *Clinical Behavioral Medicine in Small Animals*. Philadelphia: Mosby, 1997.

Owens, Paul. *The Dog Whisperer: A Compassionate, Nonviolent Approach to Training*, 1st ed. Cincinnati: Adams Media, 1999.

Pitcairn, Richard, and Susan Hubble Pitcairn. *Dr. Pitcairn's Complete Guide to Natural Health for Dogs and Cats*, 3d ed. Emmaus, PA: Rodale, 2005.

Pryor, Karen. *Don't Shoot the Dog: The New Art of Teaching and Training*, rev. ed. New York: Bantam, 1999.

Rugaas, Turid. *On Talking Terms with Dogs: Calming Signals*. Wenatchee, WA: Dogwise, 1997.

Schoen, Allen, DVM, and Pam Proctor. *Love, Miracles, and Animal Healing*. New York: Simon and Schuster, 1995.

Yin, Sophia. *How to Behave So Your Dog Behaves*. Neptune City, NJ: T.F.H. Publications, 2004.

———. *Low Stress Handling, Restraint and Behavior Modification of Dogs and Cats*. Davis, CA: CattleDog Publishing, 2009.

Index

About the Author

Alana Stevenson is a professional dog and cat behaviorist, humane dog trainer, and animal massage therapist who consults nationally and internationally. She helps people resolve their pets' behavioral problems using humane, nonviolent approaches grounded in science and learning theory. Alana has been involved in animal advocacy, protection, and rescue for over two decades, and she encourages people to adopt animals in shelters. She shares her home with a myriad of four-legged animal companions — all rescued.

She is a professional member of the Animal Behavior Society, the Association of Animal Behavior Professionals, the Association of Pet Dog Trainers, and the International Association of Animal Massage and Bodywork. Her articles on humane dog training and behavior modification have appeared in *The American Dog*, *NOVADog*, *Animal Wellness*, and the UK-based *K9* magazine. She can be contacted through her website, www.alanastevenson.com.